TO DIE FOR

Mörderische Kurzkrimis

zum Englischlernen

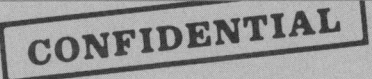

von Dominic Butler

PONS GmbH
Stuttgart

PONS
TO DIE FOR

Mörderische Kurzkrimis

zum Englischlernen

von Dominic Butler

1. Auflage 2016

© PONS GmbH, Stuttgart 2015
Alle Rechte vorbehalten

PONS Online-Wörterbuch: www.pons.eu
E-Mail: info@pons.de

Projektleitung: Francesca Giamboni
Autor: Dominic Butler
Redaktion: Brian Wolfe
Korrektorat: Natalie Gaab
Einbandgestaltung: Anne Helbich, Stuttgart
Logoentwurf: Erwin Poell, Heidelberg
Logoüberarbeitung: Sabine Redlin, Ludwigsburg
Layout: Petra Michel, Gestaltung & Typografie, Essen
Satz: Datagroup Int. SRL, Timisoara
Druck: Publikum d.o.o.
PONS verpflichtet sich, den Zugriff auf die zu diesem Buch
gehörige Vokabeltrainer-App mindestens bis Ende 2019 zu
gewährleisten. Einen Anspruch der Nutzung darüber hinaus
gibt es nicht.

ISBN: 978-3-12-562818-2

Dominic Butler

Dominic Butler stammt aus Nordengland. Er ist Englisch-
lehrer und Schriftsteller. Nach seiner Schulzeit, die er an einer
klassischen Grammar School (entspricht dem deutschen
Gymnasium) verbrachte, studierte er Film und Literatur an
der Sheffield Hallam University. Während seiner Studienzeit
arbeitete er in Teilzeit als Gerichtsschreiber am Strafgericht
in Sheffield. Dort erwachte sein Interesse für Kriminalfälle,
die von nun an Thema vieler seiner Kurzgeschichten wurden.
Dominic lebt und arbeitet zurzeit in Italien, wo er Englisch
unterrichtet und gerade seinen ersten Roman beendet, einen
düsteren, jedoch humorvollen Krimi.

EINIGE WORTE VORAB ...

Sie lesen gerne Krimis und möchten etwas für Ihr Englisch tun?
Mit diesen spannenden Kurzkrimis tauchen Sie noch tiefer in die Sprache
ein und erweitern Ihren Wortschatz. Die verwendete Sprache passt
genau zu Ihrem Lernniveau, so dass sie die richtige Mischung aus neuen
und bekannten Elementen bietet.

Nicht nur Krimis lesen, sondern auch mehr
über Land und Leute erfahren:
Im Anschluss zu jeder Geschichte finden Sie
wissenswerte Informationen zu den **Schau-plätzen**, an denen die Geschichten spielen.

Schwierigere Wörter
sind auf jeder Seite
in den **Fußnoten**
übersetzt. Im Anhang
können Sie nochmals
alle Wörter in
einer alphabetischen
Wortliste
nachschlagen.

Wo die einzelnen Schauplätze liegen, können
Sie in der **Weltkarte** auf den Seiten 6 und 7
nachschauen.

Alle Wörter, die in den Fußnoten übersetzt sind, können Sie
mit der **PONS Vokabeltrainer-App** üben. Gehen Sie einfach auf
www.pons.de/kurzkrimis-en und laden Sie die App kostenlos auf Ihr
Smartphone oder Tablet herunter oder üben Sie online.

INHALTSVERZEICHNIS

- -

1.	SIX FEET UNDER	8
2.	CAUGHT RED-HANDED	15
3.	LIKE FATHER, LIKE SON	23
4.	THE GREEN-EYED MONSTER	30
5.	MURDER WILL OUT	37
6.	MURDER IN THE ICE	44
7.	A ROCK AND A HARD PLACE	52
8.	NO SMOKE WITHOUT FIRE	60
9.	LITTLE WHITE LIES	68
10.	WHAT DOES NOT KILL YOU	75
11.	A SKELETON IN THE CLOSET	82
12.	TO DIE FOR	89
13.	OUT OF THE FRYING PAN	97
14.	MURDER IN THE DARKNESS	104
	WORTLISTE	118

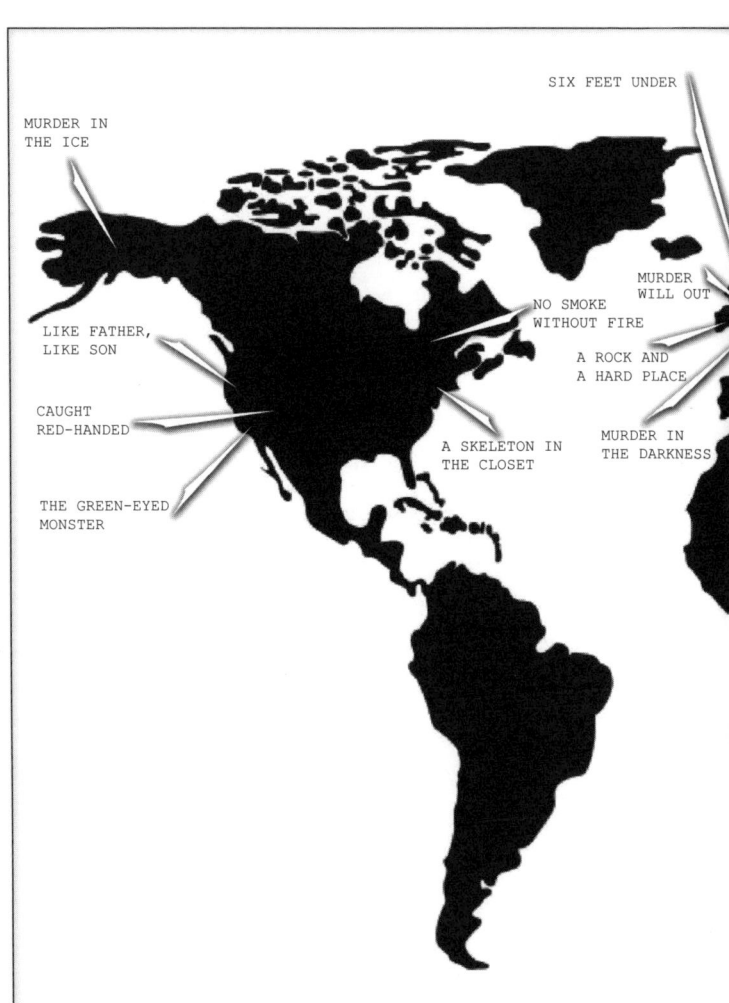

MURDER IN
THE ICE

SIX FEET UNDER

MURDER
WILL OUT

LIKE FATHER,
LIKE SON

NO SMOKE
WITHOUT FIRE

A ROCK AND
A HARD PLACE

CAUGHT
RED-HANDED

A SKELETON IN
THE CLOSET

MURDER IN
THE DARKNESS

THE GREEN-EYED
MONSTER

LITTLE WHITE LIES

OUT OF THE
FRYING PAN

TO DIE FOR

WHAT DOES NOT
KILL YOU

1. SIX FEET UNDER

The angel was in her dream again; however, this time her steel face was that of an old and angry man. The eyes were filled with hate, and the voice with the sound of vengeance[1].

But it was just a dream.

Except this dream seemed to be so much more real than any other. This dream felt cold. This dream was dark. This dream was hard against her back and head.

No, she did not like this dream; so she forced her eyes open.

Normally, her room was light, even at night, because for many years now, she had hated being in places where she could not see. Yet tonight the room was filled with an impenetrable[2] darkness, and she felt a sudden stab of fear.

She quickly tried to move her arm to reach the lamp on the bedside cabinet, but instead her elbow banged[3] against something hard, and she cried out.

Confused, she tried to sit up, but this time her head struck[4] something.

Panic spread over her. The type of panic you feel when you wake in the middle of the night, sweat covering your body, your heart beating, your mind still half-convinced that the monster of the nightmare is a reality.

She kicked her legs, but they too seemed to be trapped. Only then did she begin to form an image in her mind of where she was.

---

1 **vengeance –** *Rache*
2 **impenetrable –** *undurchdringlich*
3 **to bang against sth. –** *gegen etw. stoßen*
4 **to strike sth. –** *gegen etw. schlagen*

An image of a small space, enclosed on all sides, virtually[1] no bigger than the length[2] and width[3] of a person.

The image of a coffin[4].

The sound that escaped from her lips was horrendous[5] to hear. It did not sound like a woman at all. It sounded like a wounded[6] animal. It sounded like fear itself.

"Help me!" she screamed, her voice muted by the small space. "For God's sake, somebody help me! Help me! There's been a mistake! Get me out of here! Get me the hell out of here!"

After several minutes of screaming and kicking and trying to hit her hands against the wood, she stopped. Slowly she managed to regain some control of herself, to stop the tears that were falling down her face, to slow her breathing and to start thinking.

The first thing she did was check her clothes. They seemed to be the same suit and blouse that she had been wearing when she left the restaurant.

The restaurant. Was that the last thing she could remember? No, she could remember walking home through the city of Newcastle.

So what had happened? An accident?

Despite her fear she was still an intelligent woman. No, there had been no accident. At least, not of the physical kind. The cut on her head was the only part of her that hurt right now.

Right now? What time was it right now?

Her watch, it had luminous hands[7]! If she could…

But before she moved her arm, she knew that the watch was not there. For more than ten years she had worn that watch. Now its very absence[8] made her begin sobbing again.

---

1 **virtually** – *praktisch*
2 **length** – *Länge*
3 **width** – *Breite*
4 **coffin** – *Sarg*
5 **horrendous** – *entsetzlich*
6 **wounded** – *verletzt*
7 **luminous hands** – *Leuchtzeiger*
8 **its very absence** – *eben ihre Abwesenheit*

"Damn it, Jean!" she told herself. "Pull yourself together[1]. You can get out of this. Think!"

Her watch was gone. That could only mean one thing.

That someone had placed her in this coffin in spite of the fact[2] they knew she was still alive.

Her heart began to race[3] again, but this time it was anger that drove it. "You cowards!" she screamed.

Her phone? No, if they had taken her watch, they would have certainly taken that.

So she was alone.

Her family would never know what had happened to her, though they would be full of the suspicions[4] that had tormented them for years. It was the fear of every judge's family: the fear that one day a criminal would take revenge[5] upon the person who had delivered their justice.

In the dark she began to cry again, and this time she made no attempt to stop herself.

"Judge Grey?" a quiet voice whispered. "Can you hear me?"

Judge Jean Grey jumped in shock, her head banging against the wood once more. The voice was quiet and muted, but it seemed to be very near to her. "Who is that? Where are you?" she shouted.

"Judge Grey, if you can hear me, you have to find the walkie-talkie. Can you do that? Can you reach down and find it? Somewhere near to your right leg."

The judge's right hand quickly searched in the dark and found something. It was a thick plastic square, and she could feel large buttons on it.

"Press the first button if you want to speak."

1 **to pull oneself together** – *sich zusammenreißen*
2 **in spite of the fact** – *trotz der Tatsache*
3 **to race** – *pochen*
4 **suspicion** – *Verdacht, Misstrauen*
5 **to take revenge upon sb.** – *sich an jdm. rächen*

For a moment the judge waited. She tried to compose[1] herself, to remove the fear and tears from her voice. When she finally pushed the button, it was the voice of the famous crown-court[2] judge that spoke. The judge who had brought to justice more criminals than any other in the north of England. The judge who was famous for her tough sentences and iron rulings[3]. "Listen to me. Listen very carefully. I don't know who you are. I don't know why you are doing this. I only know that you are making a very big mistake. Do you really believe that you will not be found? I'm a crown-court judge. Someone will have seen you take me. Someone will be looking for you even now. Let the authorities know where I am, and I'll call for them[4] to be lenient[5]. Fail to alert them, and I'll make sure you suffer for this."

There was a long silence; then the quiet voice spoke again.

"You don't like the dark, do you? You don't like small dark places?"

It was horrible to hear her phobia on the lips of this man, but she was determined to be strong. "What do you want? Money? I have money, but the only way you can get it is to get me out of here now. You may have my wallet, but I'll never tell you the pin code."

"9784," the voice said quietly. "I know all of your secrets, Judge Grey. I know it all. I know where you hide the cigarettes that you tell your husband you don't smoke. I even know why you're scared of the dark, but I want to hear you say it."

The judge's blood turned to ice. This was not the voice of a petty criminal[6]. This was the voice of a madman[7]. "Look, you

---

1   **to compose oneself -** *sich zusammennehmen*
2   **crown court -** *Strafgerichtshof*
3   **ruling -** *Richterspruch*
4   **to call for sb. to do sth. -** *jdn. auffordern, etw. zu tun*
5   **lenient -** *nachsichtig*
6   **petty criminal -** *Kleinkrimineller*
7   **madman -** *Verrückter*

have to listen to me. I'm a good person. I've done my job for the good of society. If I've sentenced you or one of your family, it was in the name of the law." Verurteilt

Another silence. "Yes, you've been a good person. Not all your life, but for the last fifteen years. Before that, though…"

"So why are you doing this to me?" she shouted.

"Judge Jean Grey," the voice said. And suddenly the judge remembered hearing the voice as she walked past an alley on her way home. She had turned and seen the face of an old man, but then a needle had pressed into her neck, and she had felt herself falling.

"You drugged me!" betäubt

"Yes. I learnt all about drugs just for this day. Like I learnt all about you. I watched you. I followed you, for nearly fifteen years. I could have killed you a hundred times. In a way I became you. I became your judge. And this… this is your sentence." Urteil

"Who are you?" the judge screamed. And she banged her head against the wood of the coffin and felt soil[1] falling between the gaps, soil that made her realise how real this was. How there really was no escape.

"No. Maybe not a judge," the voice said. "Something else. Maybe an angel."

The angel. Every day for fifteen years she had thought about that angel. Every time she had driven past the statue she had tried to look away.

"No. Please, not this." zu fauchen

"Yes, this," the voice hissed. "Fifteen years ago you were leaving your golf club after another extravagant dinner, and you were drunk. You crashed your car on the Durham road, hitting another car and killing the driver. You were trapped in your car, in the dark, alone. I don't know if you could see it: the Angel of the North, the statue looking down on you as you

---

1 **soil** – *Erde*

betteln

alles zu vertuschen

cried and begged for mercy[1]. I only know that when the family of the dead driver asked for justice from the courts they found none. You used your power and influence[2] to cover it all up. You never confessed that it was your fault. The other driver, a young woman, was dead, but you were never punished. Now this is your punishment, Judge Grey."

Bestrafun bestraft Fault

The judge screamed and shouted and hit her fists against the wood. "I'm sorry! It's true! It's all true. It was my fault. That poor girl. I killed her! God forgive me! But please, don't leave me here! I've tried to make things better, I've tried to be a good person."

When she stopped speaking, there was a quiet sigh, and then the voice spoke for the final time. "That's all I ever wanted to hear you say. Ever since the day you killed my daughter."

For a moment there were no other sounds than the judge's sobbing, but then there was a strange noise above her, and the wood seemed to creak[3].

Schluchzen provisorisch

Tentatively she raised her hands and pushed the lid[4] of the coffin, soil and dirt falling into the gaps and covering her. She screamed in fear, fear that the soil would suffocate[5] her; then she pushed harder, and this time the lid fell back, and the early morning sky was revealed.

Sarg

Slowly she tried to stand, her legs weak, and her eyes unbelieving[6].

Her coffin was buried in no more than half a foot of soil; the large stone that had been on top of it was lying on the grass.

And the giant statue of the Angel of the North was standing above her, justice and vengeance on her steel face.

1	**mercy** – *Gnade*	
2	**influence** – *Beziehungen*	
3	**to creak** – *knarren*	
4	**lid** – *Deckel*	
5	**to suffocate** – *ersticken*	
6	**unbelieving** – *ungläubig*	

Engel des Nordens, England

Auf einem Hügel in Gateshead, Nordengland, steht seit 1998 die 20 Meter hohe Statue eines Engels. **The Angel of the North**, entworfen von Antony Gormley, besitzt 50 Meter lange Flügel, welche die Statue für Zugreisende auf der Ostküstenhauptlinie zwischen London und Edinburgh sehr deutlich sichtbar machen. Der Künstler sagt über die Statue, dass sie an die Bergarbeiter erinnern soll, die an dieser Stelle über 200 Jahre lang – und in der umliegenden Region mehr als 500 Jahre – in der Dunkelheit gearbeitet haben. Darüber hinaus solle der Engel eine freundliche, beschützende Wirkung ausstrahlen, die durch die Haltung seiner Flügel vermittelt werde: Sie sind leicht nach vorne gewinkelt und deuten eine Umarmung an.

2. CAUGHT RED-HANDED

The body lay on top of the hot red rocks.

It was almost impossible to see that it had once been a person. Now it was only ruined flesh[1], broken bones and blood.

The park ranger kneeling in the sand and rock some metres from the mess removed her hat and used it as a fan in front of her face in an attempt to stay cool.

It was no good. It was nearly two o'clock in the afternoon, and the sun was high above the Grand Canyon, its blistering[2] rays shining down on the scene.

She looked up at the clear blue sky above the cliffs and shook her head. The fall that had killed the person must have been at least from ten thousand feet, she thought.

"Not a nice way to go[3]," she said, quietly, watching the fly that had noticed the body and thinking about what she should do next.

Suddenly, behind her, she heard a footstep. She turned, her hand moving to the pistol on her belt.

"Sorry," the man said, his face shocked.

He was tall, dark-haired and disquieting[4]. Something about the way he stood there made her think that he had been there for some time. That maybe he had wanted to let her know he was there by placing his booted foot heavily on the floor. He was wearing a pair of khaki pants,[5] a red and black lumberjack shirt[6] and a rucksack that was fastened over his shoulders. He looked

---

1	**ruined flesh –** *zerfetztes Fleisch*
2	**blistering –** *glühend*
3	**to go –** *sterben*
4	**disquieting –** *beunruhigend*
5	**pants –** *(AE) Hose*
6	**lumberjack shirt –** *Holzfällerhemd*

exactly like the type of hiker that she expected to find out in the canyon at this time of year.

So why did she think he was not what he seemed?

"Who are you?" she inquired, her hand still on the gun.

"Jesus, what… what is that?" he asked.

Ranger Clarke stood up slowly, her eyes carefully assessing[1] him from behind her reflective sunglasses. "Do you know what this is? Does it have anything to do with you?" she probed, her tone neutral, yet beads of sweat[2] forming on the palm of the hand that was holding the gun.

He shook his head, his eyes never leaving the horrific corpse behind her. "No… no, I… God, is that what I think it is?"

He seemed to have no idea what was going on. Still, there was something about him that she did not quite trust. "What are you doing out here?"

He continued to stare at the bloody mess behind her, and she began to feel her patience disappearing. "Answer me. What are you doing here?" and she unbuttoned the leather strap[3] that held her gun in place.

"Hey, what? Look, I'm Zac… Zac Dee, I'm just hiking, you know, the rim-to-river trek[4]."

"Have you got any I.D?" she asked.

He nodded, his eyes still on the corpse. "Yeah… I have it here…" and he began to step forwards, but then suddenly he staggered[5] and fell.

Despite her mistrust[6] she quickly moved to catch him, putting her shoulder under his arm and helping him sit down and remove his rucksack. "You're okay," she said, the same

---

1   **to assess sb. –** *jdn. mustern*
2   **bead of sweat –** *Schweißperle*
3   **strap –** *Riemen*
4   **rim-to-river trek –** *Wanderung vom Rand des Grand Canyons zum Colorado River*
5   **to stagger –** *schwanken*
6   **mistrust –** *Misstrauen*

words she had said to at least a dozen heat-exhausted hikers. "You need some water."

He shook his head. "It's not that, it's… God, how can you look at that thing?"

She smiled in spite of the situation. "Not a big fan of blood?"

He shook his head and took the bottle of water from his belt. "I hate it. We should call the police."

She nodded. "I already did. They should be here in a while. They told me to just wait. So that's what I'm doing."

"Did you see, you know, what happened?"

"Nope[1]."

"It looks like he's fallen right out of the sky."

She looked around. This part of the canyon was wide, the Colorado River two or three miles to the east. It was not a location that hikers normally came to as they preferred to follow the water.

"People don't just fall from the sky," she said, wondering[2] again if he was who he said.

He looked up. "Sure they do. Parachutes fail to open. People fall out of those little tourist planes. They have those around here, don't they? Maybe there was an accident in one. Or maybe a husband and wife had an argument, and the wife pushed him. Or…"

"Okay, enough," she said, taking her own water and drinking deeply.

He nodded. "Sorry, I get talkative[3] when I'm nervous."

She thought for a second. "No worries. Look, if you're feeling okay now maybe you should keep moving. I can wait here for the police. There's nothing you can do to help."

1   nope – *nö*
2   to wonder – *sich fragen*
3   talkative – *gesprächig*

Zögert

He <u>hesitated</u>, and her feeling of mistrust returned. The man claimed that he hated the sight of blood, yet he seemed in no rush[1] to get away from the body.

Who was he really?

"I can't just go. I'd feel bad about leaving you. I mean, what if this wasn't an accident. What if there's someone out here watching us right now?"

Watching us right now? Yes, she almost felt like there was. Did he have a friend hidden in the shadows of the rocks, a pair of binoculars[2] aimed at her face?

She had to think quickly.

"Don't worry me," she said, tapping the gun at her waist. "If you want to help, head down to the river and follow it south. You'll probably see the police. Send them in my direction."

He nodded. "Well, if you're sure?" he said, standing up and picking up his rucksack.

She looked around the canyon, her eyes searching for a reflection that meant someone was watching.

There was none.

As he turned back to her, she hesitated for a second. "I'm sure," she said.

Then she pulled her gun from her belt and shot him in the chest.

The sound was not too deafening[3] within the canyon, as it was not a high-calibre gun. Still, she had shot him directly in the heart, and he fell back into the dirt without another word.

Shame[4], she thought as she put the gun back. The idiot was just in the wrong place at the wrong time.

---

1   **to be in no rush** – *es nicht eilig haben*
2   **binoculars (pl.)** – *Fernglas*
3   **deafening** – *ohrenbetäubend*
4   **Shame.** – *Wie schade.*

She turned back to the corpse. She knew what she had to do, although the idea made her stomach heave[1].

She took a handkerchief from her pocket and tied it around her face. Then, moving quickly, she walked to the bloody mess then leant down[2] and plunged[3] her hands into the flesh and guts.

"Jesus Christ!" she protested, her stomach retching[4] at the ghastliness[5] of the deed[6]. "Where is it? Where the hell is it?"

Finally her fingers touched something, and she pulled her hands free, blood dripping from them like paint.

But it didn't matter because she had it. A black plastic tube no bigger than her two largest fingers. It seemed ridiculous that such a small thing could be so expensive, but the Mexican cartel said that it was the prototype of a new drug that would change the world. Stronger than cocaine, purer than opium. Not that she cared about all that. All that mattered to her was the ten million dollars she would receive for taking it to her contact in New York.

She wiped the blood from it with the sleeve of her ranger's uniform, looking with distaste[7] at the stupid green jacket that she had worn for the last eight years.

Had she ever liked the job? Maybe, but not anymore. She wanted a better life than all this. She wanted a house by the ocean, a yacht to relax on and servants to look after her.

She would go back to the Jeep, bring the canister of petrol and burn the two bodies. Then she would go, leave the stupid canyon and never look back.

"Put your hands up, Clarke," a voice said from behind her. She tensed, her hand hovering[8] over the gun at her belt.

---

1   **to heave** – *würgen*
2   **to lean down** – *sich beugen*
3   **to plunge sth. into sth.** – *etw. in etw. hineinstecken*
4   **to retch** – *würgen*
5   **ghastliness** – *Grässlichkeit*
6   **deed** – *Tat*
7   **distaste** – *Abneigung*
8   **to hover** – *schweben*

"Don't even think about it. I don't intend on being shot twice in one day. Turn around."

She raised her hands and turned. He was standing in front of her just like he had been when she first saw him. Except now his rucksack was by his feet, and a gun was in his hand. There was blood on his head from where he had fallen, but none on his chest where she had shot him.

"Yeah," he said with a cold smile. "In spite of your best efforts[1], I'm still alive. And now, Caroline Clarke, you're under arrest for receiving drugs with the intention to transport. Also, for attempted murder[2]."

"I knew you weren't who you said you were!" she shouted.

"I'm exactly who I said I was: Zac Dee. I just didn't mention that I'm also an FBI agent. We've been watching you for some time, Clarke. We knew the cartel was looking for someone reliable in the States. Looks like they made the wrong choice. I wanted to speak to you, to see if you would work with us to help close down the cartel. But that was before I saw the body and before you attempted to murder me."

In the distance the sound of a helicopter racing across the canyon could be heard. And somewhere near the river was the sound of a police siren. The loose-fitting lumberjack shirt had nicely covered Agent Dee's bullet-proof vest[3]. Now it was the wire[4] under the same shirt that had done its job.

"No! You can't do this," she said. "You don't understand: they'll kill me. The cartel – they'll find me in prison and kill me."

The cop looked at the bloody mess behind her. "You know, I think you're probably right, but there's not much I can do about that. There's not a judge in the whole country that will

---

1   **effort** – *Bemühung*
2   **attempted murder** – *versuchter Mord*
3   **bullet-proof vest** – *schusssichere Weste*
4   **wire** – *Wanze (Abhörgerät)*

declare you innocent. You have heard the expression 'caught red-handed', haven't you?"

She looked at her hands. The blood was drying quickly in the sun, and her skin was now the colour of the rocks that surrounded the canyon.

"But tell me," he said, "why this elaborate way of dropping[1] the drugs? Who was this? Why did they kill him?"

"I don't know," she said, tears filling the eyes behind her sunglasses. "They just told me to be here. They said they were dropping the stuff today. That it was going to be nicely wrapped so that it wasn't damaged…" She turned back to look at the body one more time. "And that there would be a message reminding me not to make any mistakes."

CAUGHT RED-HANDED

---

1   **to drop (off) sth. –** *abliefern*

Grand Canyon, US-Bundesstaat Arizona

Durch den Fluss Colorado in die roten Steine von Arizona geschnitten, ist der **Grand Canyon** als eines der sieben Weltwunder der Natur bekannt. Diese gigantische Schlucht erstreckt sich über 445 km, ist an ihrer schmalsten Stelle 6 km und an ihrer weitesten Stelle 32 km breit. Sie erreicht eine Tiefe von bis zu 1800 m. Je tiefer man in den Canyon hinabsteigt, desto älter wird das Gestein. Während die oberen Schichten erst 270 Millionen Jahre alt sind, entstand das Gestein an den tiefsten Stellen der Schlucht bereits vor 1,84 Milliarden Jahren. Der Nordrand des Canyons befindet sich im Durchschnitt auf 2400 über dem Meeresspiegel, weswegen es hier im Winter schneien kann. Die menschliche Besiedlung dieses Gebiets datiert etwa 12.000 Jahre zurück. Heutzutage teilen sich fünf Völker der Ureinwohner Amerikas das Land um den Canyon: die Paiute, die Havasupai, die Hualapi, die Navajo und die Hopi. Im Jahre 1908 wurde der Grand Canyon zum Nationaldenkmal und 1919 zum Nationalpark erklärt.

3. LIKE FATHER,
LIKE SON

"Is he dangerous?" she asked, watching as a guard with a grim[1] face emptied her bag onto the table.

For a moment he did not reply, but then he looked up at her with an expression of distaste in his eyes. "This is Folsom Prison, lady: of course he's dangerous."

She felt a knot of anxiety twisting in her stomach, but she tried not to show it.

"Don't listen to him," a younger guard standing by the door to the interview room said. "Old Owen's a teddy bear compared to some of them. He's never any trouble. He does what he's told. You'll be fine."

The first guard turned and looked at the second, his dark eyes angry. "What do you know about him?"

The other shrugged. "He seems okay to me."

"Okay?" The first guard shook his head. "Yeah, well that's because you don't have a clue[2] what that sick maniac did." He turned back to her. "But you do, don't you? And now you want to write more stories about him. Did you ever think that the reason these psychopaths do what they do is because of the attention that the newspapers give them?"

"Leave her alone[3]," said the other guard. "It's her job."

"Well? Do you know what he did to those children?"

She swallowed and nodded her head. "Yes, but…"

"Yeah, that's what I thought." He put her things back in the bag and passed it to her. "You do not go past the blue line. You

---

1 **grim –** *düster*
2 **not to have a clue –** *keine Ahnung haben*
3 **to leave sb. alone –** *jdn. in Ruhe lassen*

do not give anything to the prisoner or take anything from the prisoner. You do not take photographs of the prisoner, and any recordings will be copied and given to us. Do you understand?"

"Yes."

He turned to the other guard. "She's all yours," he said then walked away without a second look.

"Ignore him. He's always like that," he said as he opened the door. "There's nothing to worry about. If you want to get out, just shout, I'm right here."

As she stepped into the small white room, she did not know exactly what she was expecting, but the man sitting at the table, his legs chained[1] to the floor, and his wrists[2] to the table, was not it.

He must have been about fifty years old. His hair was as white as snow, his face lined with worry and regret[3], his eyes soft and blue like a summer sky.

Was this really the man she had read about?

"Mr Owen, my name's Julie Cliff. I'm from the Californian Star. Do you know our newspaper?"

The man looked at her for a moment then shook his head. "I don't read the newspapers, Ms Cliff: there's nothing but misery[4] in them."

She looked at the chair that had been prepared for her, positioned at the table and behind the blue line that the guard had mentioned. For a moment she hesitated.

"Please, sit down if you like. I don't know what you want from me, but I don't get to see many new faces, so you are welcome." His voice was gentle and polite.

She nodded, walked to the chair and sat down. "Thank you. And thank you for allowing me to speak to you."

nickle

1   **chained** – *angekettet*
2   **wrist** – *Handgelenk*
3   **regret** – *Reue*
4   **misery** – *Elend*

He smiled a little. "The warden[1] was quite insistent[2]. He said he wanted the world to see how his prison could reform a convict[3]. Even…" he said letting his eyes look down at his hands. "Even a convict like me."

The small white room was warm, yet his words sent a cold shiver down her back. "I see. Well, maybe the warden has not entirely understood the significance of my visit."

His eyes narrowed a little, and he shook his head. "I won't talk to you about… about things from the past. I've been in this prison for eleven years. I've been atoning[4] for those things. You can't ask me about that again," he said, his voice rising a little.

"It's okay, Mr Owen. I don't want to talk to you about that. Not exactly. I would like your help with something."

He stared at her in silence for a moment then nodded. "If I can help, I will."

She took a file from her bag and placed it on the table. "Mr Owen, there have been two crimes committed in the last six months. Very serious crimes. A young man called Daniel Lane and a young woman called Debbie Spencer were killed in Sacramento. Daniel was twenty-two, Debbie twenty. They were both killed in the same way."

"That's… terrible," the convict said. "But how can I help you?"

"You can look at the photos."

There was a strange tension in the room for a moment, as though[5] Mr Owen knew exactly what the photos would show.

"Okay, if you think I can help," he said finally, with fear in his soft voice.

---

1 **warden** – *Gefängnisdirektor*
2 **insistent** – *eindringlich*
3 **convict** – *Verbrecher*
4 **to atone for sth.** – *für etw. büßen*
5 **as though** – *als ob*

She slowly opened the file, her eyes watching his face and the shock and disgust[1] that slowly appeared on it. "Do you see why I think you can help, Mr Owen?"

For a moment Mr Owen was silent, but then a low and horrible moan[2] escaped from his lips. "No! No! Not that. Don't show me that!"

The door to the room quickly opened, and the young guard entered. "Is everything okay here?" he asked, his hand moving to the radio at his belt.

"It's okay," she said.

"It's not okay!" Mr Owen groaned, turning his head away from the pictures. "It's not!"

"Mr Owen, you said that you wanted to help. These people, they're about the same age as your son Billy, aren't they? Don't you want to stop the person who did this? Stop someone hurting people like Billy?"

The sound of his son's name seemed to silence him, and after a moment he nodded, though tears had risen to his eyes.

The guard looked at her questioningly[3].

"It's okay," she said then watched as he left the room and closed the door again. "Mr Owen, I don't want to upset[4] you. I've read the reports about your crime. I know that you have always said how sorry you were for what you did."

"I… I was… I am. It was a terrible thing."

"The police don't believe me, but I think that there's a copycat killer[5] somewhere in Sacramento. Someone who is trying to recreate your crimes. You saw the mouths of the victims. They were… ripped[6]. Just like the mouths of the four children… that were found in your basement."

---

1 **disgust –** *Ekel*
2 **moan –** *Stöhnen*
3 **questioningly –** *fragend*
4 **to upset sb. –** *jdn. durcheinander bringen*
5 **copycat killer –** *Nachahmungstäter*
6 **ripped –** *zerrissen*

Tears began to fall down Mr Owen's face, but he nodded his head. *Opfer*

"Mr Owen, you never explained why you did that to your victims. I think that maybe if you could tell me that now, it might help the police to find the type of person who committed these horrible crimes. And you want to help, don't you? You want to help the young people like your son?"

"Yes," he said, quietly. "I would do anything for Billy…"

"Does Billy come to visit you, Mr Owen?" she asked, thinking that maybe his son's name would encourage him to speak a little more. *artworkle*

"No," he replied, shaking his head. "No. He lives with a foster family[1] in Washington. It's better… better if he's there."

She nodded. "I understand."

He moved his head to look at the pictures one more time, tears still rolling down his face.

"So? Can you tell me why you did that? Why you ripped their mouths?"

When he spoke again his voice was strange and distant. "I don't know… I think…I think the rips made them look like they were… smiling," he said.

"Smiling?" she asked, another cold shiver running down her back.

"Yes, like they were happy. Like it was all just a game."

She was silent for a moment. "Why did you want them to smile?"

He looked at her then, more tears escaping from his gentle eyes. "Everyone needs friends," he replied quietly. Then a scream escaped from his lips, and he began to kick the table and pull at the chains holding his wrists. "Everyone needs friends!"

The door to the interview room opened again, and this time the first guard entered. "That's it! The interview is over."

---

1 **foster family –** *Pflegefamilie*

unerträglich

"But why, Mr Owen?" she tried to ask, the sound of his screams almost <u>unbearable</u> to hear.

"You've got your story, now get the hell out of here", the guard shouted, pulling her up and pushing her out of the room.

The younger guard came forward and gently took her arm to escort her along the corridor to the exit. "Are you okay?" he asked.

"Yes," she said, her heart beating strongly. "Just… God… I don't know… he seems so fragile. I almost can't believe he could ever do anything so terrible."

"Yeah. I know what you mean."

They reached the next security door and stopped as they waited for it to open. "Does he ever have any visitors? He said he doesn't get to see many new faces."

The guard shook his head. "Not many, just the son. He's been coming every week for the past few months. Strange kid. Quiet. They don't even talk really. It's like the old man can't look at him. The guilt[1] I suppose."

She turned to him, a horrible feeling rising in her chest. "The son? Billy? But he's in Washington with his foster family."

"Not anymore. He's twenty-one now. He moved back to Sacramento half a year ago. But like I say, he's a bit strange. I can't imagine he's made many friends."

"What?" she asked as the door opened.

"Yeah, you know, he's a bit odd[2]. But then maybe that's what happens when your father is convicted[3] of murder."

She stopped before the door, her mind racing, her memory of the old newspaper stories returning to her.

"No," she said. "No, he was always like that. The reports said he didn't say a word as they took his father away. That he never even asked why. He was in the house the day the kids were killed. In his room."

---

1 **guilt** – *Schuldgefühl*
2 **odd** – *seltsam*
3 **to be convicted of a crime** – *eines Verbrechens überführt werden*

The guard shrugged. "Yeah, well, like father like son[1], I suppose."

No, not like father like son, because the father seemed so gentle, so kind. Then Mr Owen's words returned to her. "*I would do anything for Billy...*"

Folsom Prison, US-Bundesstaat Kalifornien

1880 öffnete das **Folsom Prison** 32 km entfernt von Sacramento, Kalifornien. Das Gefängnis wurde besonders durch ein Konzert bekannt, das Johnny Cash 1968 hier für die Gefängnisinsassen veranstaltete. Sein berühmter Song „Folsom Prison Blues" war allerdings schon über ein Jahrzehnt früher entstanden. Folsom Prison ist eines der ersten Hochsicherheitsgefängnisse der Vereinigten Staaten. In seinen Anfangszeiten mussten die Häftlinge 7,5 Stunden am Tag ohne Mittagessen in einem Steinbruch arbeiten. Heute fertigen die Insassen die Kennzeichen aller in Kalifornien zugelassenen Fahrzeuge und stellen Straßenschilder her.

LIKE FATHER, LIKE SON

1   **Like father like son.** – *Wie der Vater, so der Sohn.*

4. THE GREEN-EYED MONSTER

As she stood at the bar waiting for the drinks, she caught[1] her reflection in the mirror behind the bottles of spirits. Her short red hair was striking[2], her deep brown eyes undoubtedly attractive. In any other town she would have been called beautiful.

This, however, was not any other town[3]. This was the only town that mattered[4]. The only place on the planet that mattered.

This was Hollywood.

In this town there were two types of beautiful. There was the type that sold movies, and there was the type that did not.

Zoe had been here for eight years now. Eight years of slowly realising that she was that second type of beautiful.

Sure, her girlfriend said she was a goddess, but what did her opinion matter?

In the reflection behind her, she saw Heather waiting patiently at their table, a script[5] in her hands and her eyes occasionally glancing around the bar, an unconscious[6] action allowing her to see how much attention her raven-black curls and to-die-for[7] figure were attracting.

And she was attracting a lot of attention.

"Is that your friend?" the barman asked as he put the drinks down. "Is she in something? I recognise her. That medical series?"

1	**to catch sth. –** *etw. erblicken*
2	**striking –** *markant*
3	**not any other town –** *nicht irgendeine Stadt*
4	**to matter –** *von Bedeutung sein*
5	**script –** *Drehbuch*
6	**unconscious –** *unbewusst*
7	**to-die-for –** *unwiderstehlich*

Zoe shook her head, put twenty dollars down and gave him a look that said "shut up." The barman seemed to understand, but even as he walked away he continued to look at Heather.

Moths[1]. They were all moths, and Heather was the light.

She looked at herself in the mirror again. There had been a seed of doubt in her mind for a moment, but the barman's question had washed it away. Quickly, making sure that no one could see, she dropped[2] the five crushed pills[3] into one of the drinks and shook it, watching with curiosity as they dissolved.

Then, fixing her smile into place, she turned and walked back to the table. "Here you are," she said, placing the drinks on the table.

"Okay, but this is the last one. I want to be fresh for tomorrow."

"It's only soda water," Zoe laughed, watching as her friend put the glass to her full red lips and drank.

"Yeah, but…"

"What? Are you still not feeling well?"

Heather shook her head. "I don't know, it comes and goes. These last few weeks have been awful. I keep getting these moments of… well, anyway, I feel great now."

"Good, I'm glad[4]," Zoe said, raising her own glass. "I know how much you want this part."

Heather shook her head. "I feel awful even trying for it. You're the one who found it first."

"Don't be silly[5]. To be honest I don't think I'll even go. Lucy wants to take me for lunch at some expensive restaurant. It's one of our anniversaries." The lie came easily to her lips. She had practised saying it over and over as she had driven to the bar. Lucy was away all weekend visiting her brother; this meant she could complete her plan in peace.

---

1 **moth** – *Nachtfalter*
2 **to drop sth.** – *etw. fallen lassen*
3 **pill** – *Tablette*
4 **glad** – *froh*
5 **Don't be silly!** – *Red keinen Unsinn!*

"Oh great! You know how bad I'd feel if I took another part from you."

The words were said innocently enough, yet Zoe felt a knot of anger twist[1] in her stomach. "No, really," she said, hoping the resentment was hidden from her face. "You'd be much better for it than I would."

She looked at her friend. Yes, she did not look as amazing as she usually did. The dark make-up could not truly hide the dark rings beneath Heather's eyes. The relaxed smile could not completely hide the nervousness that the pills had slowly encouraged.

This was the fifth time that Zoe had spiked[2] her friend's drink in the last three weeks. Each time she had increased the amount[3]; each time she had carefully watched to see the effects.

She did not want to hurt her friend of course: only make her a little anxious, a little ill, perhaps.

Was it even a crime? Zoe doubted it.

Despite the drugs, however, Heather still seemed determined to go to the audition[4].

To Zoe's audition.

Had she been angry the first time that Heather had taken a role meant for her? A little. The second time, though, had really hurt. Sure, it was only a small part in a second-rate movie, but it had been Zoe's part.

And this time? Well, this time was different. This time the part was fantastic. She had read the script and fallen in love with it straight away[5]. This role was hers.

And no one was going to stop her from getting it.

After twenty minutes of talking about the usual Hollywood gossip, Heather began to seem a little quiet. "Is everything okay? You look a little pale," asked Zoe.

---

1 **to twist** – *sich drehen*
2 **to spike a drink** – *etw. in einen Drink tun*
3 **amount** – *Menge*
4 **audition** – *Vorsprechen*
5 **straight away** – *sofort*

"No, it's fine. It's just a little hot in here. I think I might go home."

They walked to their cars together, and Zoe watched the way her friend seemed to sway[1] in her black heels. For a moment that seed of doubt touched her again. Could she really let her drive home like this? Her house was in the Hollywood hills, and the roads were infamously[2] dangerous.

"Are you sure you're okay?" she asked.

"I'll be fine. I just need a good night's sleep. I'll be okay for the audition."

My audition, Zoe thought, the anger returning. "Well, you take care[3]. And Heather – good luck for tomorrow," she said with a cold smile.

She got into her own car and watched as Heather slowly drove away. Then, making sure she was not too near, she began to follow her.

The Hollywood sign was high above the town, the white letters like a beacon[4] in the hot and humid night.

She knew that her friend was right about being fine by the morning. The pills would be out of her system by then, her composure would have been regained and her beautiful, movie-selling looks once more intact.

Beside Zoe, on the passenger seat, were the items[5] that she had purchased[6] the day before. She had hoped that she would not have to use them, but now that it looked like Heather would still go to the audition, she knew that they were her only choice.

In front of her she saw Heather's car swerve[7] around another sharp bend, and an oncoming[8] car flashed its lights.

1	**to sway** – *schwanken*
2	**infamously** – *berüchtigt*
3	**You take care.** – *Pass auf dich auf.*
4	**beacon** – *Leuchtfeuer*
5	**item** – *Gegenstand*
6	**to purchase** – *erwerben, kaufen*
7	**to swerve** – *ausscheren*
8	**oncoming** – *entgegenkommend*

For a second Zoe's heart stopped as she thought there would be a collision.

That would be too terrible. Heather did not deserve that.

Did she?

As they reached the elegant apartment in the hills, she slowed her car and waited as Heather parked and staggered to the door, her car keys shaking in her hand.

There were no lights on in the apartment.

So Zoe waited, watching as the lights in each room were turned on, picturing[1] her friend moving from the kitchen to the lounge and from the lounge to the fashionable bedroom with its glass doors that looked out over the town.

Finally, all the lights were turned off again.

It was time.

Zoe picked up the strange items and looked at them, a cruel smile coming to her face. All she wanted to do was scare her fabulous, beautiful, audition-stealing friend. The knife that she held was a fake, the metal no sharper than the edge[2] of a table. The mask which she had chosen was ridiculous, the red skin of a strange monster no better than a kid's Halloween costume.

But the eyes…the eyes were curious. Two big green circles that seemed to be laughing in a dark and malicious[3] way.

Yes, they would scare Heather. The pills would have made her half-delirious by now. All she had to do was push her a little further, and she would either not sleep at all or face a night full of terrible nightmares. And her audition would be ruined.

Hiding the mask and knife beneath her jacket, she left her car and moved quickly around the back of Heather's apartment.

Only when she was in the shadows beneath the trees did she put the mask on her face and take the knife in her hand.

---

1   **to picture sth. –** *sich etw. ausmalen*
2   **edge –** *Kante*
3   **malicious –** *bösartig*

Slowly enjoying the sensation of anticipation[1] growing in her stomach, she approached[2] the glass doors of the bedroom. The night was so humid that Heather had left them open, and the curtains were gently swaying in the breeze. Through the light material Zoe could see a figure lying on the bed in the semi-darkness.

This was it. This was where her movie career would really begin. All she had to do was enter the room, lift the knife and scream. It would be a horrible image for anyone, but for Heather's drugged imagination it would be a horrific scene[3].

She pulled back the curtain, jumped into the room, raised the knife and opened her mouth…

But the scream never came.

She pulled the mask from her face, and her hand dropped the knife.

"I… I forgot… I forgot that she was coming tonight…" Heather said as she crouched[4] in the corner of the room, her car keys still in her hand, blood dripping from the metal.

Her eyes were vacant[5], her voice slurred[6] by the drugs. She did not even seem to understand who Zoe was.

But Zoe did not care. She finally found her voice as she recognised the unmoving body on the bloodied bed. The naked body of the woman who had fallen asleep waiting for Heather's return and who had been unprepared to fight off the frenzy.

The woman who had said that she was away all weekend visiting her brother.

"Lucy!" she screamed as she fell to her knees. And the sound drifted out across the hot night of the Hollywood hills.

1   **anticipation** - *Vorfreude*
2   **to approach sth.** - *sich etw. nähern*
3   **a horrific scene** - *ein Bild des Grauens*
4   **to crouch** - *kauern*
5   **vacant** - *ausdruckslos*
6   **to slur sb.'s voice** - *jds. Stimme undeutlich machen*

Los Angeles

Um der Vormachtstellung der Thomas Edison Motion Picture Patents Company in New Jersey zu entkommen, begannen Filmemacher in den frühen 1900er Jahren nach **Los Angeles** zu ziehen. Die idealen Wetterbedingungen, das abwechslungsreiche Gelände und die Aussicht auf Arbeit ohne weitere Eingriffe von Edison machten Hollywood zum perfekten Niederlassungsort für Filmproduktionsfirmen, wie beispielsweise die Biograph Company.

„In Old California", ihr erster Film, wurde in Hollywood produziert. Nachdem sich die Begeisterung der Biograph Company für diese Gegend herumgesprochen hatte, zogen bald weitere Filmemacher nach Los Angeles um. Das berühmte Hollywoodschild wurde 1923 aufgestellt, um ein neues Wohngebiet nahe dem Gipfel von Mount Lee zu bewerben.

5. MURDER WILL OUT

Above the granite-grey mountains of the Scottish Highlands, storm clouds were slowly moving across the dark skies of another cold winter night.

In the deep valleys and quiet towns below, the clouds' approach seemed to bring with it a growing sense of danger. Yet, in an old hunting lodge[1] on a quiet road between two silent hills, this sense of impending doom[2] was muted[3] by drunken voices, laughter and the sound of wine glasses being brought together.

"To us! And to another year of good business," a man of about sixty years with a dark beard and large smiling eyes said. Around the table the other dinner guests raised their glasses.

It was an elegant room. The table was dressed in white cloth, and the light was provided by more than twenty candles placed in delicate silver holders.

"How about another bottle of wine, Hamish?" the man with the dark beard and smiling eyes asked.

At the head of the table, a younger man with a pale face shook his head. "I think it's time for the port, Mac," he said, signalling to the butler who stood silently by the door.

"Good idea!" Mac replied.

"The port please, Bill," Hamish politely said to the elderly butler. "Then you may leave us for the night."

The master of the house and the servant exchanged a long and serious look. "If you are sure, sir?"

---

1   **lodge -** *Hütte*
2   **sense of impending doom -** *Vernichtungsgefühl*
3   **to mute -** *dämpfen*

Hamish nodded, and the butler moved away, returning with a dusty bottle of port.

"Looks like good stuff," said Duncan, the red-headed man to the left of Hamish.

"It's... special," Hamish replied. Then he watched carefully as the butler took the cork from the bottle and filled the twelve small glasses around the table. "Not yet, Anne," he said, as he saw an attractive middle-aged woman lift the glass to her lips. "I would like to make a toast first."

Hamish watched the butler leave the room and close the large oak[1] door. Then he stood, his glass of port in his hand, and he looked around the table.

Duncan, Col, Sandra, Anne, Kevin, Beth, Mac, Pete, Chris, Mike and Sally. Eleven people that he had known for more than ten years. Some of them, like Mac and Kevin, he had known since he was a child. Many of them he had considered part of his family, and all he had considered friends.

But what were they now?

"I would like to make a final toast tonight. You all know me: you all know that I am a man of few words. However, today, as I am sure you all know, is the anniversary of my father's death[2], and I would like us to raise a glass to him and to wish him peace."

The atmosphere in the room changed so quickly that it seemed like a window had been opened and the storm had been allowed to enter.

"To your father," said Mac.

"Yes, to Douglas, a good friend and a great businessman," said Kevin.

"To Douglas," Anne agreed, and everyone around the table nodded their heads or gave their own quiet toast[3].

---

1 **oak –** *Eiche*
2 **death anniversary –** *Todestag*
3 **toast –** *Trinksrpuch*

Hamish nodded, looked at them, and then drank. Around the table eleven other glasses were lifted to lips, and everyone shared in a moment's silence as they tasted the dark port.

Only when he was sure that everyone there had tasted the rich fortified wine[1] did Hamish speak again. And when he spoke, his voice was deeper, louder, more filled with some dark and terrible meaning. "Murder… will… out[2]."

The three words hung in the air around the table.

"What?" Kevin finally asked, his normally relaxed expression replaced by uncertainty. "Why would you say that, Hamish?"

Outside, the rain began to fall more heavily, and the wind screamed around the lodge, but inside there was only the crackle[3] of the candles and silence as they waited for Hamish to reply.

"Why? You all know that these were the final three words that my father said. You all know that in this very house[4] he fell to the floor in his room and died. Some of us were here. Duncan, Col, Sandra, Anne, Mac, Pete. Others had left and were driving home. But only hours before, we had all been here together. When he fell to the floor we heard his screams, and we ran to his room. His face was already blue, his eyes red with blood, but as he lay there on the floor we all saw him raise his hand and point to me, his only son. Then he said those three words, words which I have not stopped thinking about from that day to this. 'Murder… will… out.'"

Mac shook his head. "Yes, we were there; we saw it, but that's all over now. We all know that you had nothing to do with your father's death. We know you loved him."

Hamish nodded. "Yes, you were all very supportive. We told the police what he had said, but you all agreed that it was a

---

1   **fortified wine** – *Dessertwein*
2   **Murder will out.** – *Der Täter wird erwischt. / Die Wahrheit wird herauskommen.*
3   **crackle** – *Knistern*
4   **in this very house** – *in ebendiesem Haus*

mistake: the dementia of a sick man. But then someone sent a letter to the police. A letter that said I was guilty, that I had planned to kill my father to inherit[1] his money and his business."

"A horrible joke. Or some competitor[2] trying to ruin the business. We all know that," said Sandra.

"Someone from another oil company. It's obvious," agreed Pete.

"Yes, that's what we thought. So I told the police that I would help them in any way that I could. That they could interview me, search my office, search my home."

"But there was nothing to be found, because you were innocent," said Sally.

Hamish moved from the table to stand at the window. For a moment he watched the rain before turning back to the eleven people. "It's true. There was nothing there when the police searched my home. But that is only because my butler, Bill, found the poison[3] that killed my father before the police arrived."

There was a stunned[4] silence.

"What do you mean? Your father died of a heart attack," said Anne.

"Yes, Anne, a heart attack caused by a poison."

Kevin stood up and shook his head. "What are you saying? This makes no sense! The doctors found nothing in Douglas's blood."

"That's true, Kevin. However, I believe that was only because the person who killed my father did not know about all of the medication he was taking. One of the prescribed[5] drugs hid the poison."

---

1   **to inherit sth. -** *etw. erben*
2   **competitor –** *Konkurrent*
3   **poison –** *Gift*
4   **stunned –** *verblüfft*
5   **to prescribe –** *verschreiben*

"I don't understand anything you're saying," said Sally. "Why was there poison in your house?"

Hamish sat back down at the table. "Because the killer wanted the police to think that I was guilty. They wanted to frame[1] me for my own father's murder. If Bill had not found the poison, I would now be in prison."

"But why would someone do that?"

There was a flash of lightning from the storm outside, and Hamish smiled. "Is it not obvious? Think about my father's last words."

Duncan shook his head. "Murder will out?"

"Yes. I thought he was saying that the guilty person would be discovered. That the crime would be revealed. But I was wrong. My father was a clever man, cleverer than I am. Even in those last moments he knew that if I was found guilty of murder, I would be out of his will[2]. Murder... will... out. Out... of his will! He knew that someone had wanted me to lose control of the business... and he knew that it was someone in this room."

Some of the guests stood. "You can't be serious?" asked Mac.

"Oh, but I am. I have never been more serious. I have thought about it for a year. The killer must be one of you. You were all here the night of his murder. Any one of you could have poisoned his drink. And all of you own shares of the business. All of you would be rich if you took control."

The eleven people began to look around at the others' faces. "But who? Who was it?" cried Anne.

"Well, that is the difficult part. But I have a solution. A way of discovering the truth. Bill has locked the doors. None of us may leave until someone has confessed[3]."

---

1 **to frame sb. for sth. –** *jdm. etw. anhängen*
2 **will –** *Testament*
3 **to confess –** *ein Geständnis ablegen*

"What? You're joking?!" shouted Pete, who ran to the door but failed[1] to open it. "You're insane[2]! No one is going to confess. Let us out!"

"Someone will confess. You see, also, before the meal, Bill and I took the poison that killed my father and injected it through the cork of the bottle of port that we are all drinking. The antidote[3] for the poison is outside with Bill. Enough for all of us, including the killer. I only want a confession. I don't want anyone to die."

For a moment there was silence, but then chaos followed. Some of the guests stood up and shook their heads in disbelief; others began to shout and scream at Hamish. Three ran to the door and began to kick and hit it, and Duncan ran to the window and tried to smash the reinforced glass[4].

Only two people remained silent and seated. One of them was Hamish; the other was Mac. The older man with the dark beard and usually smiling eyes put his head in his hands and swore.

"What is it, Mac?" asked Hamish, and some of the others turned to look.

"You bloody idiot! You don't know what you've done!" he shouted. "There is no antidote to that poison. You've killed us all!"

Hamish waited silently for all of the other guests to understand the significance of Mac's words; then he raised the glass of port to his mouth and drank. "I know," he said. "But you see, there's no poison in that bottle either."

---

1 **to fail to do sth. –** *etw. nicht machen können*
2 **insane –** *verrückt*
3 **antidote –** *Gegengift*
4 **reinforced glass –** *drahtverstärktes Glas*

Bohrplattformen, Cromarty, Großbritannien

Zu den schottischen Seegewässern gehören sowohl Teile des Nordatlantiks als auch Teile der **Nordsee**. Die Öl-Ressourcen in der Nordsee vor der schottischen Ostküste gehören zu den größten in der Europäischen Union. Sie wurden in den 1960er Jahren entdeckt; mit der Ölförderung wurde 1976 begonnen. Das plötzliche Wachstum und die Entwicklung der Nordsee-Öl- und Gasindustrie der 1970er und 80er Jahre schaffte tausende neuer Arbeitsplätze und machte Aberdeen und seine Umgebung zu einem der wohlhabendsten Standorte des Vereinigten Königreiches.

In einem Volksentscheid im Jahr 2014 wurden die Bewohner Schottlands befragt, ob Schottland Teil des Vereinigten Königreichs bleiben oder unabhängig werden soll. Die Befürworter der Abspaltung betonten, dass ein unabhängiges Schottland eines der reichsten Länder der Welt wäre, denn der Großteil der Ölfelder liegt in schottischen Gewässern. 55,3 % der Schotten entschieden sich gegen die Abspaltung.

6. MURDER IN THE ICE

The celebration, if that is what it should be called, was slowly coming to an end now.

Most of the younger staff of Fairbanks police station had either gone home or returned to their desks to complete their shift under the warming influence of a large whisky or two. The older staff, however – the ones who had known Ken Hooper since the early days – were standing around a table raising another glass to him.

"To Hooper's retirement! He shot like a girl, drank like a girl, but he sure as hell knew how to crack a case[1]!" said Detective Hutch, a big red-headed man with more than a few streaks[2] of silver in his beard.

Around the table three other men raised their glasses to Hooper, and the centre of attention, a short balding man with a plain and honest face, nodded his head and raised his own glass. "Thanks for speaking about me in the past tense already, Hutch. It'll be you next, you know."

The men laughed. "Maybe," said Hutch. "But not for a while yet. I'm still in my prime[3]. Speaking of which[4], if any of you are thinking about going home, I'll get the chief to put you up for retirement too. There's still many a tale[5] to be told about old Hooper here."

Hooper shook his head. "I don't know, Hutch. I still have a bit to get sorted out here."

---

1 **to crack a case** – *einen Fall lösen*
2 **streak** – *Strähne*
3 **to be in one's prime** – *im besten Alter sein*
4 **speaking of which...** – *da wir gerade davon reden, ...*
5 **many a tale** – *manch eine Geschichte*

"No problem. Throw your stuff in a box and come meet us over at the Anchor. It's either that or we drag you there now and cuff you to the bar[1]," Hutch said with a grin.

"I guess one more won't hurt."

"Ha! One more? Do you see what I mean lads? He drinks like a girl!"

Hooper shook his head with a smile and strolled back to his office as the others pulled on their winter coats and scarves.

Stopping at the door, he looked at the small dark space.

It seemed strange to see it so empty.

He had cleared out his filing cabinets[2] and stripped the walls of the usual case files and information that he had so studiously[3] collected. Even his plants were gone, sent home with Molly, his wife, two days before.

"Thirty-five years," he said to himself, shaking his head in disbelief. Thirty-five years, and finally it was all over.

Had he ever really expected to make it to retirement? He had certainly faced his fair amount of trouble over the years. Or gone looking for it, as Molly would doubtless say.

Taking the final cardboard box, he moved around the room picking up the last items that he had to collect: an old notepad which had sat at his desk for almost as long as he had, a mug from his son with the words *Best Dad* printed on it, and a picture of himself and the guys ice fishing over in the White Mountains when their faces had been free of lines and their futures stretching out in front of them.

"A million years ago," he muttered, picking up the box.

He looked around the room once more and was about to leave when a long-forgotten memory came to him.

White Mountains.

---

1   **to (hand)cuff sb. to sth.** – *jdn. mit Handschellen an etw. fesseln*
2   **filing cabinet** – *Aktenschrank*
3   **studiously** – *sorgsam*

Slowly he put the box back down and turned around, looking at the filing cabinet as if it were the first time he had ever seen it.

Was it still there, he asked himself, knowing that the answer was yes.

And do you really want to look at it?

This time no answer appeared.

He walked slowly to the cabinet and pulled open the top drawer. Then, placing his hand under it, he felt for the file which he had placed there so many years earlier.

His heart beginning to beat faster, he took the file back to the desk, turned on the small lamp and sat down. In the station the occasional person passed along the corridor, but he knew they would not disturb him. He was just some old retiring cop lamenting[1] over the one case he had never really solved. The one case that had haunted him for years.

The one that had got away.

He opened the file and looked at the scribbled[2] notes. It had been a year after the fishing trip when they had received the call.

The report said that a black Jeep had driven past a group of fishermen on the mountain road, attracting their attention because of its speed. The fishermen had claimed that a young woman in the passenger seat of the car had seemingly been in distress[3].

Hooper and Hutch had been returning from another case and were the closest to the area. So, despite Hutch wanting to leave it to the uniformed cops to follow up, they had followed the route and had finally found the black Jeep parked in the bushes by an abandoned hunting lodge[4] which was still covered in snow and ice after a long and cold winter.

---

1   **to lament over sth. –** *über etw. klagen*
2   **to scribble –** *kritzeln*
3   **in distress –** *in der Not*
4   **hunting lodge –** *Jagdhütte*

On seeing the Jeep, Hutch's attitude had seemingly changed from one of complete disinterest to obvious concern.

Exiting their car, they had split up, Hutch taking the front and Hooper moving silently around the back to cover the exit.

Normally they had always worked well together, giving the other enough time to get into position before making a move, communicating properly.

But not that day.

No, that day Hutch seemed to forget it all. He kicked open the door before Hooper could get anywhere near the back entrance.

When Hooper heard the first shot, he dived into the snow and pulled his own gun free. The next shots came quickly, but it was obvious that they were not directed at him, so scrambling[1] to the back porch[2], he smashed open the door and moved into the room to see the scene of horror.

The young woman was clearly dead.

Her hands and legs were tied to a bed, her clothes torn from her body and a single gunshot wound in her head.

Hutch was at the door, quickly reloading his gun then firing four more shots at the Jeep as it departed along the snow-covered road.

"What happened?" Hooper asked, running to the door as the Jeep disappeared into the trees.

"I was too slow. He must have seen us. I saw him raise the gun. I kicked open the door, but it was too late." Hutch's face was pale behind his red beard.

Hooper looked around the derelict[3], half-frozen room. "How did he get past you?"

---

1 **to scramble –** *hasten*
2 **porch –** *(AE) Veranda*
3 **derelict –** *verlassen*

Hutch turned to him, his face suddenly furious[1]. "I was too slow, okay? The girl's dead. I was too slow."

Hooper nodded, not understanding where the rage came from. "We'll get him, Hutch," he told his old partner. "Don't worry, we'll get him."

But they never did.

In the empty office all these years later Hooper shook his head and sat back. It was a mystery. The man should have been easy to find. Hutch had not only seen the man's face, but they had also seen the Jeep. Yet, despite these two strong leads[2] the culprit had disappeared into thin air[3].

After six months of pursuing sightings of black Jeeps or men matching the description, Hutch had asked Hooper to forget about it. He had said that the memory of seeing the girl like that, of thinking how close he had got to saving her, was too much. He had said that he did not want to think about the man's face ever again. That he thought he would never forget that face.

Hooper had never understood, but he had put the case to one side, taping it in the filing cupboard with the intention of studying it alone some time.

"But I forgot," he thought to himself shaking his head. "How did I forget?"

"Anything wrong?" said Hutch, silhouetted in the doorway of the office.

"Hutch. I was just coming."

"Yeah, sure. I knew you'd take your time, so I thought I'd come and drag you over. What's that? Some old case?"

Hooper nodded, unsure of how to begin. "Hutch, can I ask you something? Something about that day in the White Mountain hunting lodge?"

---

1   **furious** – *zornig*
2   **lead** – *Hinweis*
3   **to disappear into thin air** – *sich in Luft auflösen*

Even in the gloom of the office it was easy to see the colour fade from Hutch's face, the good humour flee from his eyes.

"Tonight? Why?"

Hooper breathed out slowly. "Because you said you would never forget the face of the man who shot that girl. Can you do something for me? Can you describe him to me now?"

Hutch stood as still as a statue in the doorway. "That's the file, isn't it? The damn sketch is in there."

Hooper picked up the file, turned the page and looked. "Yeah, it's here. But I still want you to describe him."

Hutch shook his head. "It was thirty goddamn¹ years ago."

"You said you'd never forget that face."

For a moment Hutch was silent. Then he moved into the office and shut the door. "Yes, Hooper. I said I'd never forget the face of the man who shot that girl." Hutch looked straight at Hooper, the confession in his eyes before he even spoke it. "How could I? I see it every day in the goddamn mirror."

To Hooper the words felt like ice piercing his heart, yet he felt he had always suspected the truth. "Why? Hutch? Why did you do it? Who was he? Who was the man you were protecting?"

Hutch breathed out deeply. "My brother. My youngest brother. He was always a piece of rubbish, but when I saw him there… What could I do? I had to help him. If he had been caught, I would have been disgraced², and he would have rotted in jail. She could have identified us both. I shot her – I had to. I told him to go, to get out of town and never come back. No one could identify him. Nothing could lead back to me."

Hooper shook his head. "The identification was fake. And you didn't really shoot at the Jeep as it drove away. You should have told me, Hutch."

"Why? What would you have done?"

Hooper sighed. "Arrested you, old friend."

---

1   **goddamn –** *verdammt*
2   **disgraced –** *blamiert*

MURDER IN THE ICE

"I know," Hutch said, removing his pistol from his belt. "You always were the better cop. The better man too."

For a moment Hooper watched the gun in Hutch's hand and saw the conflict in the other man's face.

"You're a better man than you know, Hutch," Hooper said quietly, his eyes in Hutch's eyes.

For a second more Hutch stood there, but then he sighed, placing the gun on Hooper's desk.

"I don't suppose you want a last drink with an old friend, do you?" Hutch asked.

But Hooper shook his head and took his handcuffs from his belt.

Fairbanks, Alaska

Etwa 190 km vom Polarkreis entfernt liegt **Fairbanks**, Amerikas nördlichste und kälteste Stadt. Einst von Goldgräbern gegründet, ist Fairbanks heute bei Wanderern, Kletterern, Jägern und Freizeitfischern beliebt. Jeden Februar in Jahren mit gerader Jahreszahl startet bzw. in Jahren mit ungerader Jahreszahl endet hier der Yukon Quest, eines der härtesten Langstrecken-Schlittenhunderennen der Welt, das sich über 1.600 km in Kanada und Alaska erstreckt.

Wegen der unmittelbaren Nähe zur Sowjetunion wurde in Fairbanks im Zweiten Weltkrieg eine Militärbasis eingerichtet, die auch noch während des Kalten Krieges besetzt war.

Heute gilt Fairbanks als eine der Städte mit der höchsten Verbrechens-rate der U.S.A. und steht auf Platz drei der für Frauen gefährlichsten Städte des Landes.

7. A ROCK AND
A HARD PLACE

All my life, for as long as I remember, there was one thing I never wanted to be.

A gangster.

Sure, my dad was one, and my uncle was one, and they both told me that it was the only life for a MacNevin to have, but look what happened to those two.

And anyway, when they were part of the Limerick mob[1], things were different. There were rules back then. There were codes. If you were in the mob, then those guys were part of your family. You trusted them, and they trusted you, and that was that[2]. You never hurt another gang member; you never stole from him or threatened him. Being part of the mob in the old days was an honour that meant you were safe. It meant you were untouchable[3].

But all that was thirty years ago, and today things have changed. You've not just got the one crime syndicate[4] in Limerick now: you've got a handful[5] of them. Okay, so maybe some of them aren't the real deal[6], but that's not gonna stop them from blowing you away in the street.

Besides that, everything else is all messed up[7] too. The gang leaders used to be men to respect, but now they are all idiots, paranoid that their own men are gonna steal their money or put

---

1 **mob –** *Mafia*
2 **and that was that –** *und das war's*
3 **untouchable –** *unantastbar*
4 **crime syndicate –** *Verbrecherbande*
5 **a handful –** *eine Handvoll*
6 **the real deal –** *Profi*
7 **messed up –** *versaut*

a bullet in the back of their head. And there's no honour any more: you're as likely to have your throat cut by one of your own gang as by some fella[1] on the street.

Yeah, I never wanted to be a gangster, that's for sure.

So why, I ask myself, am I standing inside a bank vault[2] the size of a bathroom, a diamond as big as a rock in my hand and three psychopaths with guns staring at me?

"Jesus!" Stevie growls. "What the hell are we gonna do?"

"Open the bloody door, boy!" the boss, Grath, shouts.

"From inside? That's bloody impossible!" I say, stepping back as Stevie tries to grab me.

"What do you mean impossible?" he shouts, his face as red as his hair, and his eyes panicked.

"Look, I didn't close the bloody thing did I? It must have been your man Danny."

Grath looks towards the door, his manic green eyes furious. "Danny you worm! Open this bloody door so I can rip out your guts!"

I shake my head. "I don't think that's going to encourage[3] him to open it."

"Let me, Boss," Shane says, pointing his gun at the handle of the safe.

"No!" I yell just before he can shoot. "Are you tapped in the head[4], man? The bullet's gonna bounce back[5] and kill one of us. The metal's too hard!"

Shane turns the gun on me. His face has always reminded me of one of those ugly guard dogs, and now that his teeth are visible the similarity is striking[6]. "Tapped? You call me that again, and I'll…"

A ROCK AND A HARD PLACE

---

1   **fella** – *Kerl*
2   **vault** – *Tresorraum*
3   **to encourage sb. to do sth.** – *jdn. zu etw. ermutigen*
4   **tapped in the head** – *verrückt*
5   **to bounce back** – *zurückspringen*
6   **striking similarity** – *verblüffende Ähnlichkeit*

"Shut up," Grath says, pushing the gun down. "The boy's right. We need to be smart."

I nod my head and walk over to the door, trying to open it once more. "He's locked it for sure."

"That's it!" Stevie says, sitting down inside the safe. "I knew it was all too bloody easy for a rock[1] like that," he says with a nod to the diamond.

He's right. The whole thing was easy.

From the start I knew I could get the bank vault open: it's one of the things I do best. Still, I didn't want anything to do with it. When Grath came to see me, I told him I didn't want to be part of the gang and that my dad and uncle were both dead because of it.

Despite this convincing argument Grath made me an offer I could not really say no to: open the safe and make twenty grand, or do not open the safe, and say hello to my dad and uncle.

We got in easily enough. Danny and Stevie started to dig a hole from the building next door. They used the roadworks outside to cover the noise and stopped before they got all the way[2].

Then tonight I cut the alarm and phone lines, and we smashed our way in. Shane's next job was to stop the security guard, an old man who was so surprised that it would have been easy for us to tie him up[3]. Shane, however, decided that shooting the poor man was a better option. We left Danny to guard the hole – our only exit – while I started to work on the vault. I got it open quickly enough, and we all stepped inside.

If you've ever seen a bank vault like this, you'll know it's not that impressive[4]. There is no money placed on the floor in piles[5] like in the films, just a hundred smaller locked boxes with a load of junk[6] in most of them.

---

1   **rock –** *(ugs.) Edelstein*
2   **to get all the way –** *durchkommen*
3   **to tie sb. up –** *jdn. fesseln*
4   **impressive –** *beeindruckend*
5   **pile –** *Stapel*
6   **junk –** *Ramsch*

Stevie and Shane started smashing them all open, but Grath knew exactly where to find the diamond. Box 137. The box that had once belonged to the dead leader of a rival gang. A mobster[1] who had died after Grath and Shane had tortured him for the location of the diamond and then sliced his throat.

Easy. All so easy.

Then, just as Grath passed me the diamond so that he could check the rest of the boxes, the door of the vault closed behind us.

"That's it!" Stevie repeats. "The Gardai[2] are gonna find us in here."

"Yeah, well I'll shoot the lot of them[3] if they do," growled[4] Shane.

"What? Every guard[5] in the bloody country?"

I laugh, and Shane looks at me, his face furious. "You think that's funny?"

I think for a moment. "It is quite funny, actually," I say, before jumping back again as Shane tries to hit me.

"Leave him alone, Shane," Grath said. "He's the only one who can get us out of here."

I shake my head. "You don't break out of bank vaults: you break in! It's impossible." I stop and look at the door, shaking my head. "But just think for a minute, Grath. Why would Danny lock us in? What's the point? He doesn't have the diamond. The bloody rock's in here with us."

"He wants to take over[6] the gang! He wants the Gardai to catch me so he can be the boss."

I shake my head again. "It doesn't make any sense. He knows that even if the guards get us, you're gonna find a way to kill him. No, if he wanted to be boss, he'd have to kill you."

A ROCK AND A HARD PLACE

1	**mobster** – *Gangster*
2	**Gardai** – *irische Polizei*
3	**the lot of them** – *sie alle*
4	**to growl** – *knurren*
5	**guard** – *irischer Polizist*
6	**to take over sth.** – *die Führung von etw. übernehmen*

"And how's he gonna do that when I'm in here?"

I step in close to Grath so Shane and Stevie cannot hear. "Maybe he's not working by himself."

Grath's manic green eyes look quickly at the other two men. "You mean..?"

"Maybe. He locks us in, they wait for the right time, then… bang… a bullet to the back of your head."

Grath looks back at the other two. "Shane would never do that."

"Then it must be Stevie," I say, my eyes moving to him.

Stevie is still sitting on the floor, his head in his hands, his gun next to him. "What?" he says when he sees us both looking at him.

"Get him, Shane!" I shout, but Stevie's too quick, and his gun is in his hand before Shane can lift his.

"What is this?" Stevie shouts, keeping his gun aimed[1] at Shane as he stands up.

"You double-crossing[2] bastard!" Grath shouts.

"No, Grath, what are you talking about?!"

Shane is slowly moving his hand, the gun rising. "Now, Shane!" I shout, my voice so loud in the confined space that Stevie suddenly shoots, the bullet ripping into Shane's face, killing him instantly.

Grath tries to take his own gun from beneath his jacket, but Stevie shouts for him to stop. "Drop the gun, Grath!"

"So you are double crossing me!"

"No, you idiot, but I'm not gonna let you shoot me either!" Stevie yells.

"Idiot, is it? I'll kill you for that," Grath screams, his gun rising and firing at the same time as Stevie's.

---

1   **aimed at sb. -** *auf jdn. gerichtet*
2   **double-crossing -** *hintergehend*

The noise is like thunder, the spark from the guns blinding[1]. When I can see again Stevie is on the floor, blood spilling from his throat and confusion still in his eyes.

"Got the bastard," says Grath before he falls to the floor too.

"Grath? Grath are you okay?" I ask.

"I'm okay: he just got my shoulder. You've got to get this door open. Get us the hell out of here."

"Okay, I'll try," I say. "Here, take the diamond."

He puts down the pistol and reaches out for the rock, those manic green eyes crazier than ever. "You were right about them," he says. "You're okay, boy."

I then look at him, letting the fake concern disappear from my face. "I'm okay? Didn't you say the same thing to my dad, Grath?"

He is inspecting the crystal so carefully that he only half listens. "What? What are you talking about? I told you to get that door open."

"Yeah, you said he was okay, but you still shot him."

Grath's eyes suddenly show that he understands. He drops the rock, but his injured arm is too slow, and before he can reach the gun, I have it.

"You!"

"Yes, me. Do you know what I like about bank vaults, Grath?" I ask before he can speak. "They're soundproof[2]."

And another deafening shot fills the space.

My ears still ringing from the sound, I stand up, put the diamond in my pocket and look around at the three dead bodies.

I take my phone from my pocket and dial a number. After a few seconds I hear the mechanism of the lock, and the thick metal door of the vault opens. Danny grins as he sees me; he then looks at the dead men and laughs.

A ROCK AND A HARD PLACE

---

1   **blinding** - *blendend grell*
2   **soundproof** - *schalldicht*

"It worked!" he says. "We did it."

I take a cigarette from my pocket and light it, thinking about what he has just said.

"This is it, boy!" he says with another grin. "The gang's ours now! We can run it better than Grath ever did. Do things properly, like in the old days."

I inhale the smoke and nod my head. "Grab the other guns," I say to him; then I watch as he walks past me into the vault.

No, I never wanted to be a gangster, I think as I look at his back. But if I'm going to be one, I might as well[1] be the boss.

"Sorry, Danny. The old days are over."

And I fire a final shot before closing the door to the vault.

---

1 **I might as well...** – *Ich könnte ebenso gut...*

King John Castle, Limerick, Irland

Im gleichnamigen Gebiet des Mittleren Westens Irlands liegt **Limerick**, umgeben von einer reizvollen Landschaft und durchzogen von dem stattlichen Fluss Shannon. Während der 1960er Jahre war die Kriminalität in Limerick sehr schwach ausgeprägt. In den 70er Jahren jedoch kam es, wie in vielen anderen irischen Städten, zu einem massiven Anstieg bewaffneter Überfälle. In den 1990er und 2000er Jahren – den sogenannten „Celtic Tiger"-Jahren – stieg der Verkauf von „Partydrogen" rasant, angekurbelt vom wirtschaftlichen Boom. Über die Jahre lieferten sich in Limerick Mafiafamilien und kriminelle Banden Kämpfe um die Kontrolle über die Stadtkriminalität, die 2008 derart eskalierten, dass Limerick zur Mordhauptstadt Europas ernannt wurde.

A ROCK AND A HARD PLACE

8. NO SMOKE WITHOUT FIRE

In an office on the outskirts[1] of Ottawa, a man in dark clothes held up a glass of whisky to a picture on the wall. "Here's to you[2], Gavin," he said, before downing the drink[3] in a single swallow, the hot liquor burning in his throat.

The picture was of Gavin White, CEO of White Incorporated; the picture was of the man holding the glass of whisky. His hair was a little darker, his face a little less lined, and his eyes full of an optimism which was no longer there. But it was certainly the same man.

He filled the glass again then stared at his own portrait. How long ago had it been since the picture was taken? Ten years? Twelve?

Everything had been so different back then. His offices had been in the centre of the city, not on these forgotten perimeters[4] where there were only start-up businesses and failing companies. He had been a real player[5] back then, a name that people mentioned with admiration or envy.

And he had been rich.

Was it the loss of respect that hurt the most, or the loss of the millions that he had once possessed?

He laughed.

It was the money, of course. The rest of it could go to hell. He would trade all the respect in the world to get back half of

1   **outskirts** – *Stadtrand*
2   **Here's to you.** – *Auf dein Wohl.*
3   **to down a drink** – *ein Getränk austrinken*
4   **perimeter** – *Stadtrand*
5   **real player** – *führende Figur*

what he used to have. To own just one of the sports cars or one of the riverside apartments.

Yes, he would do anything to have his bank account full once more. To not have his credit cards declined or his loan requests[1] denied.

"You're going to get it all back," he said. "Unless you mess this up, you're going to get it all back!"

He emptied the whisky again then looked at his hand.

It was shaking.

"Be a man, Gavin! Follow the plan and nothing can go wrong."

He was about to pour a third glass, but he stopped himself.

"Later! When you're back at the hotel celebrating, you can drink."

He nodded to himself, put the bottle back in the cabinet under the picture and laid the glass down on his desk.

His plan was simple, yet brilliant.

Seven years ago, when things had started to look bad for the company, he had slowly begun to increase his insurance. He had made sure that no one had known he was losing money for as long as he could. Then he had downsized[2] to this smaller office block and waited.

For three years now he had been almost bankrupt, his assets gone, his stocks[3] failed. A less intelligent man might have thought of pulling an insurance job[4] as soon as things got bad, but Gavin knew that he had to be careful.

He had waited until people had stopped thinking about Gavin White and White Incorporated. He had waited until his now pitiful business seemed to be doing okay.

He had waited until tonight.

1   **loan request -** *Darlehensantrag*
2   **to downsize -** *schrumpfen*
3   **stock -** *Aktie*
4   **to pull an insurance job -** *einen Versicherungsbetrug begehen*

Now he was ready.

Did he care that twenty people would lose their jobs, their salaries? Did he hell![1]

This was his ticket out of here. A ticket to a condo[2] in the States, where he could drink away the rest of his life.

But he still had to be clever; he still had to be careful.

He picked up the whisky glass and walked through the dark offices. Outside the stars hung above a cold night in the city, the lights of the capital almost pleasant to look at in the darkness.

He took the glass to the kitchen, washed it then placed it back into the cupboard.

He could leave no trace to let the police know he had been here.

When they checked, they would see that he was staying at a hotel in Quebec City. Two friends would say that he was with them drinking in their hotel room all night. Two friends who would receive a small percentage of the money he would make.

He had left the hotel at midnight and driven back in a rental car then waited in the shadows of the office block.

There had been no one in the area, with only one or two lights on in the apartment block opposite[3]. In his dark clothes he had entered the building, the alarm of which he had reported damaged two days before.

So there would be no record of his entrance, no witnesses and a strong alibi to protect him.

"See, Gavin," he said to himself. "You've got this! You can do it."

He walked back to the main office where his employees worked. Fifteen computers were sleeping in the darkness. One, however, blinked a red light every few seconds.

---

1   **Did he hell! –** *Nie im Leben!*
2   **condo(minium) –** *(AE) Eigentumswohnung*
3   **opposite –** *gegenüber*

Everything was in place. He was not using matches or petrol or anything which could be detected.

He was being smart.

He had cut the electric wires in the plug of the computer. Placed the waste-paper bin next to it. Then above the bin a stack[1] of old boxes containing ink cartridges[2].

It would be the perfect accident.

He looked at his watch; it was time.

He walked over to the wire, knelt down[3] and took his lighter out. As long as he only burnt the wire, it would look like that was where it started.

He lit the lighter, a delicate yellow flame appearing above it. Then, slowly and carefully, he held it to the wire.

After a second there was a pop and a bang as the wire tore. It was on fire, the flame small but steady, licking at the waste-paper basket then quickly growing.

He stood up and clapped his hands, enjoying the sight as the boxes ignited and spread the damage.

Soon the fire alarms would activate, though hopefully not too soon.

There was one problem though: smoke. The fire had not yet spread enough to do much damage, but there was already a lot of smoke.

The window.

If he opened the window, the smoke would disappear, and the fire would still spread before the alarm went off.

He ran to the window, pushed it open and coughed as the smoke was sucked into the night.

"Yes," he said quietly. "It's working!"

That, however, was when he saw him.

---

1   stack – *Stapel*
2   ink cartridge – *Tintenpatrone*
3   to kneel down – *sich hinknien*

Standing at a window in the block of flats opposite was an old man.

For a moment Gavin froze as the old man looked directly at his face.

For a moment the old man froze too.

Then, his head coming up and his voice loud enough for everyone to hear, he shouted a single word.

"Fire!"

Gavin watched as the man took a mobile phone from his pocket and began to dial.

Smoke was everywhere now, but knowing he had to escape, Gavin ran to the door and half fell down the stairs until he reached the car park.

Inside the office the fire alarm finally began to ring, the sound causing him to panic even more.

"He saw me!" he said to himself. "He saw my face!"

God! It was all ruined. The old man would identify him to the police. They would know that it was an insurance job.

Unless…

And a dark and troubling[1] idea came to his mind.

The old man would not have described him on the telephone. He would wait and tell the police later.

But what, he thought, if there was no later?

Slowly he turned, the idea still forming in his mind, but by the time he reached the entrance to the apartments he knew what he was going to do.

And he knew he must be quick.

He looked up.

It was the second apartment on the third floor.

He opened the door to the building quickly, keeping his face hidden in case there were cameras. Then he ran to the stairs and sped up them, panic, fear and desperation moving him forwards.

---

1 **troubling** – *beunruhigend*

When he reached the third floor corridor, he checked that no one was there. Seeing that it was empty, he moved to the second door and stopped.

You can do this, Gavin.

Think of the money.

He raised his hand and knocked. "Fire department, open the door, sir," he said, not raising his voice too loudly.

After a few seconds the door opened and the old man smiled at him. "That was very quick, I only…" he started to say, but Gavin moved forwards, covered the man's mouth with his hand and shut the door.

For a second the old man was too surprised to resist[1], but then, as he began to struggle to escape, he kicked out, his knee hitting Gavin in the groin[2] so that he screamed and fell to the floor. The old man moved backwards, his hands against the walls. "What are you doing?" he shouted. "Help me! Somebody help me."

Gavin was in pain, but he was also angry now. In the distance he could hear fire engines moving in their direction, but they would not be here before he had finished.

"You're dead, old man," he said, watching as his victim retreated.

"No, stay away, I'm warning you!"

Gavin laughed. "Or what?"

The old man's right hand moved to the handle of another door which he pulled open. "Get him Maple! Kill!"

The thing that sped towards Gavin was so fast that he did not know what it was as first.

But when the teeth ripped[3] into his throat, he knew.

---

1   **to resist** – *Widerstand leisten*
2   **groin** – *Leiste*
3   **to rip into sth.** – *etw. zerreißen*

For a few seconds the dog tore into his flesh[1], but then finally the old man shouted for it to stop.

Gavin felt blood pumping from the wound, and he suddenly felt too tired to move.

"Why?" asked the old man

"You… saw me… you saw my face… saw me light the fire," Gavin said, knowing that it did not matter anymore.

"Saw you?" the old man said, breaking into a laugh, a sound horrible to Gavin's ears. "Ha! You idiot, I haven't seen a damned thing for nearly twenty years! I'm blind!"

Gavin was beginning to choke on his own blood, but he forced the words from his mouth. "Liar! You saw! You shouted fire!"

The old man laughed again, and his guide dog began to lick at the blood on the floor. "I've got a nose haven't I? I smelt the smoke. And you know what they say: there's no smoke without fire."

---

1   **to tear into sth. –** *sich über etw. hermachen*

Ottawa, Kanada

Ottawa, die Bundeshauptstadt Kanadas, wurde im frühen 18. Jahrhundert als „Bytown" gegründet. Der Name ‚Ottawa', den die Stadt 1855 erhielt, leitet sich aus der Eigenbenennung eines Urvolkes der Region ab, das aus dem Gebiet der Großen Seen stammte.

Die Stadt zeichnet sich durch ihren sehr hohen Lebensstandard und eine niedrige Arbeitslosenrate aus, die nur geringfügig von der letzten Weltwirtschaftskrise betroffen wurde. Englisch ist mit über 62% Anteil die meistgesprochene Sprache. Knapp 15% sind französischsprachig. In beiden Sprachgruppen ist Zweisprachigkeit auf muttersprachlichem Niveau eher die Ausnahme, und in der englischen Sprachgruppe ist die größte Mehrheit nur einsprachig. Diese Verhältnisse spiegeln sich in den nationalen Statistiken wider: Bundesweit sind Englisch und Französisch die Muttersprachen von ca. 57% bzw. knapp über 21% der Bevölkerung.

9. LITTLE WHITE LIES

"Tell me, was any of it true?" the woman asked, a single tear rolling from her sea-blue eyes.

The second interval was over now, and the lights in the great hall slowly faded to black.

"Would you believe me if I said yes?" the man in the suit next to her asked, his eyes never leaving her face.

A solitary female singer walked onto the stage and began to sing beneath a soft white light.

In the darkness no one could see the couple sitting alone in the private box[1] above the stage, but if they could, they would doubtless[2] have mistaken the woman's sadness for nothing more than empathy for the tragedy on the stage.

"No," said the woman, a touch of anger replacing the sadness.

"And I don't blame[3] you," said the man. "Yet it was almost all true. Ever since the first day we met, I have been honest with you about my feelings, if not about my true self[4]."

The woman shook her head, and she felt her cheeks growing warm. "Lies, it was all lies," she hissed.

For a moment the man was silent, and the singer's voice washed over[5] them. "Perhaps, but they were white lies[6]. Everyone tells white lies. This woman on the stage is pretending to be something she is not. Why can't I?"

1 **box** – *Loge*
2 **doubtless** – *sicherlich*
3 **to blame sb. for sth.** – *jdm. etw. verübeln*
4 **one's true self** – *jds. wahres Ich*
5 **to wash over sb.** – *jdn. überschwemmen*
6 **white lie** – *Notlüge*

She turned to him, her eyes flashing cold with anger. "That's her profession!"

The man nodded. "And this is mine."

For the first time the woman looked down at the gun that he held to her side. "And does your job mean that you're going to kill me?"

For a moment the man looked like she had struck[1] him, but then he lowered the gun and put it on the vacant chair to his right. "I would rather die than hurt you. Catherine…"

"Don't you dare[2] call me that! Not now!"

He smiled sadly. "Lady North, I never thought that I would fall for you[3] like this, but I have. It was never my intention."

"Then what was your intention, Mr Stone, or whatever your real name is?"

"My name is Mark, just like I told you. Stone is just a cover. One of many. And my intention? Well, this was my intention: for you to invite me to share this box with you tonight."

"Why? What are you going to do?"

Mark sighed. "My job, like I told you. My job meant that I had to be here tonight. I learnt about you several months ago. I discovered that you reserve this box every time Medea plays at the Albert Hall. Why is that? Is it because it was the last opera you saw before your parents…"

"Say another word about my family, and I'll scream," Lady Stone hissed.

On the stage the female lead[4] had been joined by a tenor, and his deep tones added a sense of dread[5] to the hall.

"Forgive me. I should leave you now," Mark said, and for the first time the woman turned to look at his face. The face that she

---

1   **to strike sb. –** *jdn. schlagen*
2   **Don't you dare! –** *Wage es nicht!*
3   **to fall for sb. –** *jdm. verfallen*
4   **female lead –** *weibliche Hauptrolle*
5   **dread –** *Grauen*

had come[1] to love over the past seven weeks. The green eyes that she had stared into for hours each night; the dark hair that she had run her fingers through a hundred times.

"Leave? Why should I let you? You say you won't hurt me, so why shouldn't I shout for help? You're a criminal. I could call the police."

"Perhaps, but I don't think you should. It's true that I do things that are... outside of the law, but sometimes people have to. The man in the next box is an ambassador[2] from a country where wars have killed thousands of people."

"So? You intend to kill him for that? He's an ambassador. He makes no decisions for his country: he only represents it."

Mark shook his head. "No, that's not why I intend to kill him. I intend to kill him because of the three young women that he kidnapped and killed the last time he visited one of his neighbouring countries. Everybody knew that it was him, but as an ambassador he was protected, and the threat of war meant that not even the authorities[3] dared bring him to justice[4]. I work for people who need assistance with this type of thing, but I only ever work for people who are in the right."

Lady North watched him carefully for a moment. "Why should I believe you?"

He shook his head again. "Maybe you shouldn't. I'm sorry, but I have to go now. Catherine..."

"No. Just go."

He stood up. "Tell me, before I do. How did you discover I was not who I said I was?"

She turned back to the opera and silently let the tears fall once more. "Did you really think that I would not check? I'm the sole heir to my family's fortune. I received the email from

---

1 **to come to do sth.** – *dazu kommen, etw. zu tun*
2 **ambassador** – *Botschafter*
3 **authority** – *Behörde*
4 **to bring sb. to justice** – *jdn. vor Gericht bringen*

my private detective during the interval. You're not the first man to lie to me for his own gain."

"You know that's not why I lied," he said in the darkness.

"Do I? Just go! Take your gun with you."

"Why? There were never any bullets in it. I told you. I would rather[1] die than hurt you. I…"

"No," she said, stopping him before the words could leave his lips.

She focused on the stage and on the increasingly strong voices of the singers as the crescendo began to rise. The violins of the orchestra seemed to mirror the pain and anguish she felt within her own heart.

Behind her she heard the curtain to the box move, and she knew that he had left her.

Tears ran down her face more quickly now; her heart seemed to beat in time with the rhythm of the opera, and her chest rose and fell as she fought to calm her breathing.

She knew that she should call for help. Call for somebody to stop him. But she could not.

And then she heard it: the sound of muffled[2] voices in the next box. The sound of *his* polite voice offering to refresh their champagne glasses.

As the crescendo rose to its peak, she heard a dull thud[3] like someone falling to the floor, and then a scream quickly cut off before it could be heard by the audience in the hall. Then there were more sounds of a struggle[4], and she felt fear replacing her anger and misery. The thought of him being hurt was too much for her to bear, but she was frozen with fear.

She was about to stand and run to the other box when she heard the curtain open, and she turned to see him standing

1   **I would rather... –** *Ich würde lieber...*
2   **muffled –** *gedämpft*
3   **thud –** *dumpfer Schlag*
4   **struggle –** *Kampf*

there, his hand pressed to a bloody wound on his shoulder. "Catherine, I know that you'll never believe me now, but I love you," he said, his face pale.

Then there were raised voices in the corridor outside, and he turned and ran.

But I do believe him, she thought suddenly, the realisation freeing her from her fear.

I believe him… and I love him too.

She stood up as she heard feet running in the corridor. Then, without thinking, she picked up the gun that he had left, kicked off her high-heeled shoes and pushed past the curtain. To her left she could see two men moving in the direction of the emergency exit, their hands reaching for the hidden guns under their jackets.

She did not know exactly what she intended to do, but she did not have time to think. She raced after them, the pistol in her hand, and the sound of the opera in her ears. When she pushed open the door to the empty back stairs, she heard someone shouting in front of her and stopped. When she looked up, though, she saw that the two men were not looking at her but at Mark, who had fallen to the floor and was moving silently away from his attackers.

"You killed the ambassador!" the first man shouted.

"Yeah, that's true. It was about time somebody did."

The attacker swore[1], kicked Mark in the side then said something to the second man who began to move his hand towards the gun under his jacket.

"Stop!" Lady North heard herself say, the pistol in her hand rising to point at the two men. "Stop, or I will shoot."

On the ground she saw the defiant[2] look in Mark's eyes suddenly fill with fear. "Catherine…" he began.

---

1   **to swear –** *fluchen*
2   **defiant –** *unnachgiebig*

"You shut up too. You've got a lot of apologising to do, and I don't intend on letting these two stop you."

The two men watched her silently. "You won't shoot," the first one said.

"Really?" she asked, pulling back the hammer of the pistol[1]. "Are you that sure? I'm not a very good shot, but from this distance I'm going to hit one of you before you can get me," she hissed, her sea-blue eyes blazing fiercely.

For a moment none of them spoke, and there was only the sound of the opera to fill the tense silence.

Then, from inside, there was a scream, and it was obvious that the ambassador's body had been found.

"We're going now," she said to Mark. "Get up and start moving."

Mark nodded and with an effort forced himself to stand. Slowly, the gun never leaving the two men, she walked to him and put his arm over her shoulder. Then, with a final glance at the two men, she began to help him down the stairwell.

Only when they had reached the bottom of the stairs and pushed open the fire escape door did she throw the gun to the floor.

"We need to get to my car," she said, helping him to run.

"Catherine, the gun: there were no bullets in it. You did know that?" he said as they struggled to get away, the Royal Albert Hall ablaze with light behind them.

"I knew that. So?"

"So you lied" he said with a weak grin[2].

"A white lie," she said, allowing herself to smile too. "Just a little white lie."

---

1   **hammer of the pistol –** *Hahn der Pistole*

2   **grin –** *Grinsen*

Royal Albert Hall, London

→ Die **Royal Albert Hall**, von Königin Viktoria 1871 eröffnet und nach ihrem verstorbenen Königsgemahl Prinz Albert benannt, ist eine Veranstaltungshalle, die bis zu 9500 Besucher fasst. Sie ist als Wohlfahrtsorganisation eingetragen und erhält keine Gelder vom Staat.

Die Halle ist bekannt für ihre klassischen Musikveranstaltungen wie die Konzertreihe „The BBC Proms" und Opernaufführungen. Hier finden jedoch auch Veranstaltungen anderer Art statt: Seit ihrer Gründung 1997 wird hier jährlich die ATP Champions Tour abgeschlossen. Darüber hinaus öffnet die Halle ihre Türen für Filmpremieren und Popmusik-Konzerte. Eric Clapton hat in dieser Halle schon fast 200-mal ein Konzert gegeben.

10. WHAT DOES NOT KILL YOU

A light rain was falling as the police car slowly made its way along the quiet country roads, grey clouds sitting above the Whangamarino wetlands in a way that suggested they would never leave.

Constable[1] Cline watched the green landscape of forests, swamps[2] and peat bogs[3] in silence, the question forming in her mind but not quite reaching her lips.

"Go on," Detective Cole said, his hands on the steering wheel[4] and his eyes on the road, "ask me. You know you want to."

Cline looked at him. His face was serious as always, his grey eyes as unreadable as the clouds above them. He was not a man without humour, but he was also not a man to waste his words. "Okay," she said. "Do you really think he's dead?"

"Does it matter what I think? The inquest[5] has agreed to declare him dead. So he's dead."

Cline looked back at the swamps and the miles of endless wilderness. "So why are you coming out here? You don't have to. You could have sent someone else. You could have sent me."

Cline was a plain woman with intelligent brown eyes and a sincere face. The police uniform that she wore suited[6] her, though she looked forward[7] to the day she would be made a detective and could wear a smart suit like Cole.

---

1 **constable –** *Polizist*
2 **swamp –** *Sumpf*
3 **peat bog –** *Torfmoor*
4 **steering wheel –** *Lenkrad*
5 **inquest –** *Untersuchungsausschuss*
6 **to suit sb. –** *jdm. gut stehen (Kleidung)*
7 **to look forward to sth. –** *sich auf etw. freuen*

"Why do you think I'm here?" Cole asked as a wooden house by the side of a forest appeared in front of them.

She thought for a moment. "Because you want to look her in the face when you tell her."

"Maybe you're right," he said, slowing the car as they entered the driveway[1] of the isolated property.

"I am right." She had learned over the past months of working with the detective that the only way to talk to him was in the same direct way that he talked to you. "What I don't understand is why."

Cole stopped the car. The gardens around the house were wild but beautiful. Long reeds[2] rose up out of the ponds, and plants grew along the thin paths that led to the forests and the swamps.

"You saw the reports. You should know exactly why I want to see her face."

"You think she killed him."

"Why not? Thirty per cent of all murders are committed by family members. Mr Harris had no family apart from her."

They got out of the car, and Cline adjusted her uniform, a slight feeling of anxiety[3] reaching her stomach. "What should I say? I've never…"

"You've never told a next of kin[4] that their loved one is dead. Well, you don't have to say anything. Consider this a lesson, but I doubt it will be the most typical of encounters[5]," Cole said, pulling the collar of his jacket up against the rain.

As they walked towards the wooden steps that led to the porch of the house, Cline saw a woman standing at the window. She was about fifty, perhaps, with auburn[6] hair tied up in a

---

1 **driveway** – *Einfahrt*
2 **reed** – *Schilf*
3 **anxiety** – *Unbehagen*
4 **next of kin** – *nächster Angehöriger*
5 **encounter** – *Begegnung*
6 **auburn** – *rostrot*

severe knot on her head and her face devoid[1] of make-up or hospitality.

Before they reached the top step, the door opened, and Mrs Harris spoke. "I know what you've come to say, Detective, but you're wrong." And with that she turned and walked into the house leaving the door open for them to follow.

It was a simple but charming place. A fire in the corner of the room was burning gently, and there were paintings of the wetlands decorating the walls. To their right the door to the kitchen was open, and a delicious smell of stew[2] or soup filled the entire house.

"Mrs Harris, this is Constable Cline."

The older woman looked at Cline for a second then seemed to dismiss[3] her from her thoughts. "I suppose I should offer you a drink. Tea?"

"No, thank you, we're fine. Perhaps we could sit."

Mrs Harris nodded to the sofa then took an armchair opposite them and waited. "Well, say it then."

"Mrs Harris, the coroner is prepared to declare your husband dead. He's been missing now for seven months, and the conclusion made by the inquest is that he has suffered an accidental death somewhere within the wetlands. This decision allows you to claim[4] his life insurance."

Silence filled the room, and Cline felt her eyes unable to move from Mrs Harris' face. Maybe she had been attractive once, but if so, it was gone now, replaced by an ugly coldness. "No, he's not dead. I know that he's not. So I don't want that money."

Cline glanced at Cole, but his expression was impossible to read. Had he expected something else? Was he waiting for

---

1   **to be devoid of sth.** – *an etw. mangeln*
2   **stew** – *Eintopf*
3   **to dismiss sth./sb. from one's thoughts** – *etw./jdn. ausblenden*
4   **to claim a life insurance** – *Anprüche aus einer Lebensversicherung geltend machen*

something that would show she had killed her husband for the money?

"You're so sure?" the detective asked.

"I am."

"And tell me, Mrs Harris, if, as you believe, your husband is alive, would that make you happy?"

For the first time an expression other than impatience[1] appeared on Mrs Harris' face, yet it was not the anger that Cline had expected: it was a smile.

"My husband is alive, Detective, and yes, that does make me happy."

Cole shook his head. "See, that's what I've never been able to believe. Mrs Cole, the first time we met, a week after your husband's disappearance, you had a bruise[2] on your face and a cut on your lip. They were not new injuries[3]: they were maybe two weeks old. You said that you had fallen down the steps in front of your house, yet I knew that you were lying. I've seen enough domestic-abuse[4] cases to know that your husband was beating[5] you."

The smile did not move from Mrs Harris' face. "Detective, what would you know about married life? There's no ring on your finger, nor on hers," she said with a nod of the head to Cline. "You think my husband abused[6] me? He did not. Did he sometimes have to teach me lessons? Yes, he did."

"Lessons?" Cline asked before she could stop herself.

Mrs Harris' eyes turned to look at her. "Yes, lessons. In spite of all your modern city teaching, you have no idea how a real marriage works. My husband taught me more than anyone. When I made a mistake, he would teach me the right way to do something. Did it hurt sometimes? Yes. But like he always said,

---

1   **impatience –** *Ungeduld*
2   **bruise –** *Bluterguss*
3   **injury –** *Verletzung*
4   **domestic abuse –** *häusliche Gewalt*
5   **to beat –** *schlagen*
6   **to abuse sb. –** *jdn. misshandeln*

what doesn't kill you makes you stronger. And I'm strong now, oh yes, very strong."

Cline looked away, shocked by the revelation.

"Fine," Cole said. "So you let him beat you for your mistakes. And what about his mistakes? What about Lisa Pool?"

Mrs Harris stood up suddenly, her eyes blazing[1] with anger. "How dare you[2]? Get out! Go on, get out of my house!"

Cole stood too. "He was having an affair with her. She was the one who let us know that he was missing. Why was that, Mrs Harris? Why did you never call the police? Your husband goes out duck hunting in the swamps one day and doesn't come back. Did you not call because you thought he was with her, or because you knew exactly where he was… and didn't want anyone to know?"

Mrs Harris looked from Cole to Cline then shook her head, the anger disappearing as quickly as it came. "Idiots. You're all idiots. You'll never understand. Now get out!"

Cole nodded, and Cline led the way to the door, pushing it open and stepping back into the light rain.

As they walked back to the car, she could feel a pair of eyes on the back of her neck. "So?" she asked. "What do you think?"

"The same thing I've always thought. There's a capacity[3] for violence in that woman. I can feel it." He looked up at the window where Mrs Harris stood. "The thing is, Mr Harris and his abuse is probably what gave her that capacity. Maybe I should just let this one go."

Cline shook her head. "You know, maybe there's another possibility. Maybe he's not dead. Maybe they faked the whole thing together for the life insurance money."

The rain began to fall harder, and as Mrs Harris moved away from the window, Cole shook his head. "No, he's dead. I can feel it in my bones."

---

1   **to blaze** – *funkeln*
2   **How dare you?** – *Wie können Sie es wagen?*
3   **capacity** – *Potential*

Inside the house Mrs Harris listened as the police drove away then she went to the kitchen and filled a bowl with steaming hot stew. Then, taking an umbrella from near the back door of the house, she stepped out into the rain and walked slowly down the wild path that cut through the forest.

When she reached a small clearing about three miles from the house, she stopped and put the bowl down on the wet, muddy ground.

"It was the police," she said. "That Detective Cole. He's a bad one, he is. He doesn't understand anything." She picked up a large stick that was leaning against a tree. "Anyway, they've gone now. They came to tell me that I can claim the insurance money." She shook her head. "And he talked about… her."

Mrs Harris moved to the middle of the clearing where there was a small peat bog. In the centre of the bog, a large piece of wood was covering something. She used the stick to move it then she smiled.

"Well, anyway, here's your dinner."

She used the stick to push the bowl out to the middle of the bog. There, with pale skin, the fat completely gone from the face; was Mr Harris' head.

As she pushed the food closer, his eyes slowly opened, and his lips moved.

"How you fell into this old bog I don't know," said Mrs Harris kindly. "I guess it was God's punishment for what you did with that woman. You were just lucky that I found you."

Mr Harris' lips moved again, the eyes pleading.

"What? Kill you? Oh no. I would never do that. Remember dear, it's just like you always say, *what doesn't kill you makes you stronger.*"

Whangamarino Sumpfgebiet, Neuseeland

Das **Whangamarino-Sumpfgebiet**, das sich im Nordwesten der Nord-insel Neuseelands befindet, ist eine der wichtigsten Regionen dieser Art im Land. Es erstreckt sich über eine Fläche von ca. 72 km^2 und besteht aus Sümpfen, Torfmooren, Flüssen und Wäldern. Viele seltene oder gar nur dort vorkommende Pflanzenarten und der Artenreichtum an Wasser- und Sumpfvögeln und Fischarten bieten für viele Biologen und Vogelkundler ein spannendes Forschungsfeld. Etwa ein Zehntel des Sumpfgebiets befindet sich im Besitz der „Fish and Game New Zealand", einer Ratsvereinigung von Jägern und Sportanglern, die sich landesweit nicht nur um die Interessen der Jäger und Angler, sondern auch um den Erhalt und die Ausweitung der Artenvielfalt kümmert.

11. A SKELETON

IN THE CLOSET

In New York housemates[1] are never hard to find. You put an ad[2] online, place a few posters at the library, the local gym, a friendly corner shop[3].

By the time you get back to your apartment, the red light on your answering machine is blinking. You hit play, and you try to take notes from the mix of different accents and voices that are all trying to convince you that they are the one[4]. That they are the person who should enter your home. The person who will be living just yards[5] away from where you sleep at night.

After that you have two or three weeks of interviews: an opportunity to separate the vaguely[6] normal candidates from the crazies who seem to populate the Big Apple.

Just look up the next time you are walking down the street. Look up at all of those apartment buildings rising into the sky. Think about all of the strange people living together like rabbits. Most of them complete strangers once. Now they share a door, a space, an address, and all just because of that first ad.

That was not, however, the way that I met Suki.

It was a rainy Sunday afternoon. I remember because my hair was soaked[7] by the time I reached the coffee house on the corner. Jack was already there, with a grin on his face and a comment about my appearance.

1	**housemate** – *Mitbewohner*	
2	**ad** – *Anzeige*	
3	**corner shop** – *Tante-Emma-Laden*	
4	**to be the one** – *der/die richtige sein*	
5	**yard** – *Yard (0,914 Meter)*	
6	**vaguely** – *annähernd*	
7	**soaked** – *pitschnass*	

I remember thanking him sarcastically, and he replied *that is what friends are for*.

Friends. Yes, Jack and I were friends.

Had there been a time when I wanted more than that?

Yes.

However, that is not important. I knew that I was not the kind of girl that Jack would ever be interested in. He liked educated, artistic women whereas[1] I was just his stupid friend Maggie.

But anyway, like I said, that is not important. This is not a story about Jack and me. It is about Suki, the woman who I would meet in that warm, quiet coffee house.

"So?" Jack asked. "When are you going to advertise for a new housemate? When did Cathy move out? Two months ago? You could save a lot of money if you found someone."

I put the large cappuccino down and shook my head. "I just can't do it. I hate looking for housemates. I hate letting those strangers into my apartment."

"Cathy was okay," Jack grinned.

"You mean she was hot. She was not okay. She was filthy[2]: she never cleaned."

"Yeah, but she had a great figure."

I shook my head.

"Excuse me."

The polite voice that interrupted my thoughts belonged to an Asian lady. She was sitting on the table next to ours, and I could not remember seeing her before that moment.

She apologised for listening to our conversation then mentioned that she was looking for somewhere to live herself.

We spoke for some time. She was dressed neatly in subtle[3] colours, and her short black hair was perfectly combed. At one

---

1   **whereas** – *während*
2   **filthy** – *dreckig*
3   **subtle** - *dezent*

point I recall seeing the way that Jack was looking into her eyes, and a part of me felt a stab of jealousy[1].

Despite this moment of doubt, I knew that she was going to be my new housemate.

She moved into the apartment the next Friday evening. I was there with a bottle of champagne to greet her, yet when she arrived she explained that she was up very early the next day, so I let her unpack her things alone. When I saw her on Saturday evening, I asked her if she wanted to go to the coffee shop.

"I'm sorry, Maggie, but I have to work again tomorrow. I work a lot, to be honest: the art gallery is very busy at the moment. I'm afraid we may not see much of each other."

On Monday I went back to work, and for the next few days I almost forgot that I had a new housemate.

"So when are we going to go out for drinks?" Jack asked on the phone one night.

"I don't know. I never see her."

The sensation of living with someone but never seeing them is a very odd sensation indeed[2].

It is like living with a ghost.

I would hear[3] the sounds of the shower in the morning. I would hear her gentle footsteps in the hall and the sound of the front door opening and closing in the middle of the night. Sometimes I thought that I heard voices in her room.

A man's voice?

A familiar man's voice?

Once I even awoke[4] in the middle of the night and thought that I heard Suki shouting a name, though perhaps that was just a dream.

---

1   **to feel a stab of jealousy** – *einen Anflug von Eifersucht verspüren*
2   **indeed** – *durchaus*
3   **I would hear...** – *Ich hörte immer ...*
4   **to awake** – *aufwachen*

It continued like this for five weeks. Suki, my perfect housemate, was a ghost to me now.

Until the night that I saw the body[1].

It was nearly two in the morning, yet I was awake in my bedroom, a book in my hands and sleep impossible due to the strong coffee that I had drunk earlier that night with Jack.

When I heard the sound of the front door opening, I turned the light off quickly, although I was not exactly sure why.

My bedroom door was open slightly, no more than a crack[2], so when I saw her slowly pass my door, I knew that she could not know that I was sitting there watching in the dark.

And that was when I saw it. She moved slowly past the door, walking backwards, and in her hands she dragged a large black bag. A large black bag with what I can only say looked like bones sticking out of the top.

"It was a body, Jack!" I hissed down the phone at him early the next morning.

"Maggie, you don't know that. You must be mistaken[3]. You've not been yourself these last few weeks."

"That's because of her! Jack, you have to believe me… I…" I stopped talking and listened. I was in the bathroom, a knife in my hand and the door locked. In the hallway I could hear her steps and waited until I heard the front door open and close. "She's gone out. Where are you?"

"I'm nearly at your building."

"Okay, listen. When you get here, wait at the lobby[4]. I have to see what's in her room. If you see her coming back, call me."

"Wait, Maggie, I don't even know what she looks like."

"Of course you do!"

"No, Maggie, I…" he started to say, but I hung up.

A SKELETON IN THE CLOSET

---

1   **body** – *Leiche*
2   **crack** – *Spalt*
3   **to be mistaken** – *sich irren*
4   **lobby** – *Eingangshalle*

It had to be now.

I opened the bathroom door slowly and looked around. The apartment was silent and empty. With the knife still in my hand, I walked to the closed door of Suki's room.

"Suki?" I asked quietly.

There was no reply. I put my hand on the door and pushed.

Inside, the curtains were half drawn, the light from the window dancing around the room.

Around me a perfectly normal room.

There were pictures of her family on a table by the bed, shoes in a neat[1] row near the window, a collection of books on the shelf.

Could I have made a mistake?

I moved to the closet[2] in the corner of the room, and for a moment I hesitated before I opened it.

And there it was.

The black bag was hanging up like a dress. Inside it I could see the same bright-white bones that I had seen the night before.

"Maggie."

I screamed as I turned. She was standing right behind me.

"Suki, what is this?" I asked, my voice shrill with terror.

She looked at me with her mysterious eyes. "Maggie, this is very wrong. You aren't allowed to enter my room." She moved towards me, and I stepped back, the knife behind me. "This is a skeleton, Maggie, from the art gallery. I use it for my drawings." She opened the bag further and revealed where the bones were held together by metal.

"Oh God," I said, feeling like an idiot. "I'm so sorry."

Suki just looked at me. "I think you should go now, Maggie."

I nodded and quickly left her room, closing the door behind me.

It was then that I felt the hand on my shoulder, and I turned quickly, the knife rising defensively.

---

1   **neat** – *ordentlich*
2   **closet** – *(AE) Kleiderschrank*

"Maggie!" Jack shouted as he stepped back.

"Jack, I'm sorry."

"What are you doing with a knife, Maggie?" he asked, his face worried.

"I was scared, but it's okay, you were right: I made a mistake. It was just a skeleton for her drawings," I said. "But…" I thought for a second, "why didn't you call me when you saw her coming back?"

"She's here? Maggie, I tried to tell you, I don't know what she looks like."

"Of course you do! You met her that day in the coffee shop."

"What? Maggie, are you okay? I've never met her. I've just heard you talk about her constantly for the last five weeks."

"What..?" I heard myself ask, but Jack was already pushing open the door to Suki's room.

"Maggie? I don't understand."

I followed him into the room.

The empty room.

There were no pictures, no shoes, no books.

I moved to the mirror and stopped.

And then I began to understand.

I looked into the mirror.

"Suki," I whispered, and in the reflection I saw her smile. She lifted a hand to her short black hair, and I saw the knife that she was holding.

That I was holding.

That we were holding.

Jack had never wanted me. He had always wanted an educated, artistic woman.

Well, now he could have Suki.

"Look in the closet, Jack," we said.

When he turned, we lifted the knife and moved behind him.

So, in the end Suki was the perfect housemate. So perfect that Jack never left us after that.

So perfect that he never will.

Freiheitsstatue, New York

"Give me your tired, your poor,
Your huddled[1] masses yearning to breathe free,
The wretched[2] refuse of your teeming[3] shore.
Send these, the homeless, tempest-tossed[4], to me:
I lift my lamp beside the golden door."

Diese Worte stammen aus dem Sonett „The New Colossus" aus dem Jahr 1883 von Emma Lazarus und sind in eine Tafel eingraviert, die ursprünglich am Podest der Freiheitsstatue in **New York City** angebracht war, inzwischen jedoch im Statue of Liberty Museum ausgestellt ist. Vor der Ära der Flugreisen zogen die Menschen, die aus anderen Kontinenten in New York eintrafen, auf Schiffen an der „Lady Liberty" vorbei.

New York ist heute eine der größten Metropolen der Vereinigten Staaten und eine der am dichtesten bevölkerten Regionen der Welt. Aufgrund der Vielfalt der Kulturen ist es auch die sprachenreichste Stadt der Welt: Man schätzt, dass in den insgesamt 280 Wohnvierteln der Stadt ca. 800 verschiedene Sprachen gesprochen werden.

1   **huddled** – *geknechtet*
2   **wretched** – *armselig*
3   **teeming** – *gedrängt*
4   **tempest-tossed** – *vom Sturm getrieben*

12. TO DIE FOR

"Look at this place. It's a palace," Detective Loux said, removing his hat and looking up at the elaborately-painted ceiling of the hotel's lobby. The reception was beneath a vast domed[1] roof, the type of which you would expect to find in a cathedral, not in a holiday resort. And the entire space was filled with palm trees, exotic flowers, statues of South Africa's wildlife and patiently-smiling attendants, who were ready to supply the guests with anything they might desire.

"What? You've never been here?" asked Detective Smit, opening his white shirt so that he could enjoy the cool breeze of the air conditioning.

"Of course not," Loux said with a shake of his head. "I've only ever seen it from the outside."

Smit laughed and slapped his partner on the back. "Well, you're in for a treat[2]. I say we get this thing wrapped up[3] quickly and get some drinks by the pool. You need to familiarise[4] yourself with the place. That's what a good cop would do."

Loux shook his head but smiled as they walked over to the long mahogany reception desk.

The two detectives were as opposite as it was possible to be. Loux was tall, with dark skin and jet-black[5] hair, while Smit

---

1   **domed –** *gewölbt*
2   **You're in for a treat. –** *Du kannst dich auf etwas ganz Besonderes freuen.*
3   **to get sth. wrapped up –** *etw. eingetütet bekommen (zum Abschluss bringen)*
4   **to familiarise oneself with sth. –** *sich mit etw. vertraut machen*
5   **jet-black –** *samtschwarz*

was short and fair, with a grin that mocked[1] his partner's more serious demeanour[2].

"Wrap it up quickly? You heard what the chief said. This doesn't sound like it's going to be quick."

"Yeah well," Smit said, placing a stick of gum in his mouth and beginning to chew. "The chief must have made a mistake. I bet[3] we'll be at the side of the pool by five."

They reached the reception desk, flashed[4] their badges and were told the room number.

"They could at least show us the way," Smit said as they headed towards[5] one of the lifts. "I don't even know if this is..."

The door to the lift opened, and a hotel maid in a blue uniform stepped out, a pile of towels in her hands and a smile on her mouth.

"Hello," said Smit. "Say, is this the right elevator for room 732?"

The maid looked at him with a pair of big blue eyes that Smit thought he might drown in. "No, sorry, it's the opposite tower. You need the lift over there."

Smit thanked her and watched her walk away while shaking his head. "You see that? Even the staff are gorgeous[6]. She had eyes to die for."

"Yeah sure, come on," Loux said, heading for the opposite lift.

As they reached the seventh floor, they could smell the smoke. "I hate crimes that involve fire," said Smit, taking his gum out and sticking it onto the wall. "You know why? Because I hate Marks. He's always so serious. You remember that

---

1 **to mock sth. –** *etw. verspotten*
2 **demeanour –** *Auftreten*
3 **to bet –** *wetten*
4 **to flash sth. –** *etw. aufblitzen lassen*
5 **to head towards sth. –** *sich auf etw. zubewegen*
6 **gorgeous –** *umwerfend*

arson[1] case back in Rustenburg? He started shouting at me for something... I can't remember what."

Loux shook his head as they walked along the corridor. "You started smoking."

"So?"

"So the place was still covered in petrol."

Smit laughed. "Oh yeah. Ah well, good job I've quit[2]."

They reached the room. Two cops in uniform were standing outside, their faces looking unhappy. "Hey boys, what's up?" asked Smit.

"It's not nice in there, Detective," Constable Jones said.

"Ah, nothing we haven't seen before."

"I bet you've never seen this," said the other, his face pale.

"Yeah? What is it?"

Jones shook his head. "We don't really know, sir. The fire alarm went off. When security got here, the door was locked so they used their own keys to get in. There was smoke everywhere and a burning body on the bed. After they put the fire out[3], they searched the place, but there was no one else there."

Loux raised an eyebrow. "So? Obviously the murderer left before security got here."

"Well, according to the guest in the opposite room, Mr Cane..."

The door to the opposite room opened. "That's me, I'm Mr Cane," said an elderly Briton with a colonial-style white moustache. "No one left that room! I heard the alarm, and I opened my door. My wife Margery phoned reception. I did not leave this spot[4]. I tell you: no one left that room!"

"Okay, thank you, sir. One of the constables will take a formal statement from you in a minute," said Loux with a polite smile.

---

1   **arson** - *Brandstiftung*
2   **Good job I've quit.** - *Zum Glück habe ich aufgehört.*
3   **to put a fire out** - *ein Feuer löschen*
4   **not to leave a spot** - *sich nicht vom Fleck rühren*

Mr Cane shook his head. "The man was blind drunk[1]. He nearly fell into me when I saw him here in the corridor."

"When was that, sir?" asked Loux.

"About an hour before the alarm went off."

"Thank you, that's all for now." The man closed the door.

"What do we need his word for?" asked Smit. "Surely they've got cameras in all the corridors?"

"Yes, sir," said Jones. "But the video just confirms what Mr Cane said. No one came in or out of this room until security got here. They entered the room, extinguished the flames...but they were too late."

Smit shook his head. "Well then, what the hell are we doing here? We're homicide[2] detectives. No murderer: no murder. No murder: no us. Come on Loux, let's hit that bar[3] early."

The door to room 732 opened, and a serious-faced man in a green plastic suit and white gloves looked at them.

"Marks," said Loux, with a nod of the head.

"Marks," said Smit, with a look of annoyance[4].

Marks stared at them coldly, passed them face masks and walked back into the room.

"One of you stay here; one of you come with us," Loux said to the uniformed cops. Neither looked happy, but Jones nodded and followed them into the room.

The scene was horrific.

The ceiling of the room was black. The bed was a blackened mess of burnt sheets and melted mattress, with the metal springs[5] visible and pressing into the chargrilled corpse.

"Who is it? Smit asked.

"Mr Thorpe," the uniformed cop said. "American expat[1] who lives in Johannesburg. Married, no kids, a lot of money and a gambling addiction[2]. A regular of Sun City."

"The wife?" Loux asked.

"Not here. The girl at reception was pretty useful: she told me all about Mr Thorpe. He comes here three or four times a year. Always alone. Always gambling. He drinks by the pool every afternoon. Sleeps for a few hours in the evening, hits the casino at night. Then, win or lose, he finds a woman to bring back to his room. Normally the type of woman you have to pay for."

"The good life," said Smit, walking to the large windows that opened onto the balcony. "Okay Marks, tell us how he set himself on fire with a cigarette in his sleep so we can get out of here."

"I wish I could," said Marks. "But I've inspected the scene carefully; there's no obvious incendiary[3]. No cigarette, no matches, no electronics. More importantly, there was not enough smoke in this room to render him unconscious. The fire only burnt for a few minutes, but it burnt quickly. And from this initial inspection it seems the victim did not even try to extinguish the flames, nor move from the bed. To be honest, Detectives, I don't believe this man died from his burns[4]. I believe he died from the shock.

Loux looked at Marks. The man had never failed to give them an answer before, but today he seemed to be hesitating.

"So what? He just exploded into flames, but lay there until his heart failed?" asked Smit.

Jones nodded his head. "It happens. Spontaneous combustion[5]."

Smit laughed. "Yeah sure!"

---

1   **expat** – *im Ausland lebender Mensch*
2   **gambling addiction** – *Spielsucht*
3   **incendiary** – *Brandmittel*
4   **burn** – *Brandwunde*
5   **spontaneous combustion** – *spontane Verbrennung*

Loux looked at Marks. "That's just a myth, right?"

Marks shrugged. "I thought so…but it does look like that."

"That doesn't explain why he didn't move. If I was set on fire I'd dive straight off the balcony into the pool."

Loux shook his head. "The neighbour said Thorpe was blind drunk. What if he was wrong? What if someone had drugged Thorpe? There are chemicals which can paralyse a person, right, Marks?"

Marks shrugged. "Perhaps, but without an incendiary it still doesn't explain the fire."

Smit swore. "Damn it man, this is your job. Find out how he did it so we can go to the bar."

Marks gave him an angry look. "Well, Detective, maybe you could do your job and look for something flammable[1]."

Smit and Loux began to search the room, but there was nothing obvious. "What about this?" asked Loux, holding up a bottle of tanning oil.

Marks shook his head. "No, not strong enough."

"Give me that, I need a bit of colour to attract the ladies," said Smit reaching for the bottle, opening it and putting some of the contents onto his hands. "Jesus, not strong enough? This stuff stinks."

Marks looked at him then walked across the room and took the bottle. He poured a little onto his hand and looked across at Loux. "This isn't tanning lotion. It's acetone. A highly-flammable liquid."

"Ah Jesus, it's all over my hands!" said Smit.

"So this is a murder?"

Marks turned back to the body. "Perhaps. If someone changed his tanning oil for this, but..."

"What?"

"Well, it's a very risky way of killing someone."

---

[1] **flammable –** *leichtentzündlich*

"Why? What's risky about that? You just let him rub it on, and then you throw a match at the guy," said Smit, opening a drawer and wiping his hands[1] on the dead guy's socks.

"Sure, but there was no one in the room to throw a match. There was nothing here that could have ignited[2] the acetone. It's a mystery."

"Hey look, his wallet," said Smit, taking it from the drawer and opening it.

Loux moved to the window and stared out at the hotel balconies and the high South African sun that hung above the hotel. "Unless...Marks, when I was a kid back in Bela-Bela, we sometimes used to use a magnifying glass[3] to burn ants. We would[4] hold it over them until the sun was so concentrated there was a flame."

Marks walked to the window and looked up at the balconies in the tower opposite where they had already been. "It could work. The perpetrator[5] would have to wait for a long time and get the magnification of the light just right. So they'd need access to one of those higher rooms over there. But God, what type of person would do that? First, exchange his tanning oil for acetone then drug him so he lies paralysed on his bed and then ignite him, knowing that even as he burns he is still alive, still conscious. They would have to be a monster."

"Or a wife who's discovered her husband's infidelity!" Smit suddenly said, turning and holding up a picture that he had found in the wallet.

"That's the wife?"

"Yeah, remind you of anyone?" he said, throwing the picture to Loux as he ran to the balcony and desperately searched the crowds of people entering and leaving the lobby.

---

1   **to wipe one's hands on sth.** – *sich die Hände an etw. abwischen*
2   **to ignite** – *anzünden*
3   **magnifying glass** – *Lupe*
4   **we would...** – *wir haben immer...*
5   **perpetrator** – *Täter*

TO DIE FOR

Loux looked at the picture and shook his head. "What are you talking about, Smit?"

"The eyes!" his partner shouted. "Look at her eyes!"

Loux stared at the big blue eyes. "What?!"

Smit ran past him and back into the corridor. "Eyes to die for, Loux! She's got eyes to die for!"

Vergnügungskomplex Sun City, Südafrika

→ **Sun City** ist der Name eines Luxushotelresorts in Südafrika nahe der Stadt Rustenburg. Das Resort wurde 1979 eröffnet und befand sich bis zum Ende der Apartheid innerhalb der Homelands von Bophuthatswana. Homelands waren Gebiete, die vom Regime Südafrikas geschaffen wurden und in die die schwarzafrikanische Bevölkerung zwangsumgesiedelt werden sollte; international waren die Homelands nicht anerkannt. Die Vereinten Nationen setzten einen Boykott gegen Südafrika durch, um die Politik der Apartheid zu verurteilen. Ungeachtet dieses Boykotts traten viele berühmte Künstler in Sun City auf. Das veranlasste den Musiker Steven Van Zandt, 1985 das Projekt „Artists United against Apartheid" zu gründen und den Song „Sun City" zu schreiben, in dem sich die Künstler gemeinsam gegen einen Auftritt in Sun City aussprachen.

13. OUT OF THE FRYING PAN

The heat was blistering[1].

The leather seats of the old sports car were so hot that they were painful to touch. The two-litre bottle of water on the dashboard[2] was nearly empty, the liquid inside virtually boiling under the refracted rays of the Australian sun.

"Why the bloody hell did we have to meet out here?" Duggie asked for the fourth time in an hour. He was a big man, heavily muscled and possessing a fat belly that was half covered by ugly tattoos. His face was wide and unintelligent, his eyes dull[3] and his bald head currently dripping in sweat.

Beside him Stu swore.

Stu was a much thinner man with shallow cheeks, dark hair and a cruel mouth. Despite the almost unbearable heat in the car, his face was bone dry[4], which was a matter of great pride to him, as he was renowned for his ability to keep cool in even the most baking Australian climates.

This could not be said, however, for his ability to keep his temper[5]. "I bloody told you! I've bloody told you three times. They want us scared, you idiot! They want us sitting here sweating, looking out at the desert and wondering if we're gonna end up under it."

"Yeah?" asked Duggie, looking out of the open window. "Well it's bloody working."

1   **blistering –** *glühend*
2   **dashboard -** *Armaturenbrett*
3   **dull -** *stumpfsinnig*
4   **bone dry -** *knochentrocken*
5   **to keep one's temper -** *Ruhe bewahren*

The sports car was a small island of white paint and rusty metal within a sea of sand, bush and mirages[1]. All around them, for as far as the eye could see, was the Great Sandy Desert. The rough country road that they had followed for more than two hours was the only indication of civilisation, the constant buzzing of flies the only indication of life. Alice Springs was more than forty miles away now, and the isolation was as intense as the heat.

"And they're late. Didn't they say two? Are you sure this is the right place?"

"Of course I'm sure you moron[2]! We went past that old broken-down bus two miles back." He felt his anger growing, so he took another cigarette from his pack and lit it, the hot, dry smoke filling the car. "They want to be late. They want us sitting here nervous, worrying and sweating. And look at yourself! You're like a bloody pig."

Duggie took a filthy white handkerchief[3] from his pocket and wiped it across his face. "It's good to sweat: it keeps you cool."

"Yeah? Well you must be bloody freezing."

In the distance, in the haze[4] of the heat mirage, they suddenly saw a small dark shape, and they stopped talking. Stu's hand moved slowly to the automatic pistol on his leg, and Duggie watched nervously.

For a moment there was a tense silence in the car. The cigarette smoke and the flies filled that silence, and the heat seemed to magnify it, and yet even then Stu did not let a single bead[5] of sweat form on his forehead.

The mirage shifted, and the small dark shape was revealed: a skinny, half-starved[6] kangaroo. It continued its quick approach

---

1   **mirage –** *Fata Morgana*
2   **moron –** *Depp*
3   **handkerchief –** *Stofftaschentuch*
4   **haze –** *Dunst*
5   **bead –** *Schweißtropfen*
6   **starved –** *ausgehungert*

towards the car for another few bounds[1] before it abruptly stopped, its head coming up and its eyes suddenly wide and fearful. Then, as if it knew that the two dangerous criminals in the car were watching, it turned and headed back towards the horizon.

"It's not them," Duggie said.

Stu looked at him with disdain[2]. "Oh, do you really think so?" he said, his voice full of aggression.

In the lock-up[3] in Adelaide, Duggie had been a useful bodyguard. Since they had been out, however, Stu had begun to feel that the big man was bad luck. All three of the jobs they had done had failed. The bank job was a disaster, they had nearly been caught by the police for the burglary, and the last job resulted in a black eye for Stu.

Still, without that last job they would not have been able to arrange this meeting with the infamous[4] Alice Springs drug dealer called "The Snake."

The job had been to rob a small-time[5] criminal operating back in Adelaide, but when they had broken into his apartment, he had been there with two members of a local gang. There had been a fight, and Stu had grabbed a bag of cash that had been on a table. It was only when they had got out of the city and had been celebrating that they had realised that the money had been fake, but it had been too late to turn back, and they had decided to leave Adelaide and the south until things calmed down.

Now they were here, with twenty thousand dollars of counterfeit money[6] and with only one chance to do something with it.

"Do you remember the plan?" he asked Duggie, his eyes scanning the horizon.

---

1 **bound** – *Sprung*
2 **with disdain** – *verachtungsvoll*
3 **lock-up** – *(ugs.) Gefängnis*
4 **infamous** – *berüchtigt*
5 **small-time** – *mickerig*
6 **counterfeit money** – *Falschgeld*

"Sure. It's simple."

"Don't just say 'sure'! Tell me what the plan is."

Duggie shook his head. "You've told me ten times. You do the speaking. I bring the money from the boot[1]. I take the coke back to the boot, and then I wait."

"Where do you wait?" Stu snapped.

"Next to the boot."

"And what do you do?"

"If they take the money, and there's no problem, I don't do anything."

"And if they realise it's fake?"

"Then I grab the shotgun[2] from the boot, and I start shooting."

Stu was about to say more when he heard the sound of an engine in the distance. It was an expensive black jeep, and it was heading across the bush straight at them.

"This is it," Stu said.

Duggie nodded, and they both got out of the car and watched as the doors of the jeep opened, and two large men in black shirts got out.

One of the men walked forward and looked at them both. "You armed[3]?"

Stu nodded.

"If you want to do business with The Snake, you put your guns on the ground."

Stu looked at Duggie. "Do what the man says, Duggie." And they both placed their handguns on the hot desert sand.

Satisfied, the men in the black shirts moved back to the jeep and said something.

"Good," said another voice, and a tall, deeply-tanned man stepped out of the jeep and smiled. He was well-dressed in a

---

1   **boot –** *(BE, AUS) Kofferraum*
2   **shotgun –** *Flinte*
3   **armed –** *bewaffnet*

light-white suit and had a cold drink in his right hand. For a moment he looked at Stu and then smiled, put the drink down on the **bonnet**[1] of the jeep and walked across to him.

"Stu? So, you're the guy who wants to buy two kilos of coke from me? Good. You never know what to expect when you arrive for this type of business meeting, but I've got a good feeling about you." For a moment The Snake looked at him closely and then nodded. "Well, look at you, Stu: you're as cool as a cucumber, aren't you? I like that. I like doing business with men with cool heads."

Stu nodded but said nothing.

"Do you know why they call me The Snake, Stu?"

Stu shook his head.

"Well, people have different ideas. Some say it's because I like to do all my important business out here in the desert. Whereas other people say that it's because if you **mess**[2] with me, if you **irritate**[3] me, if you treat me in a way that I don't like, I'll kill you." And The Snake put a hand on Stu's shoulder and smiled. "You're not going to mess with me, are you Stu?"

"No, sir. I just want to do business," he said calmly.

The Snake smiled. "Then let's do it."

Duggie brought the money over and then waited as Stu sliced his knife into the cocaine and tried it. As soon as it touched his gums, he knew it was good stuff. Great stuff **in fact**[4]. So good they could cut it a few more times and make even more money than they had hoped.

He gave it to Duggie to take back to the car and then stood patiently as he watched one of The Snake's men count the money.

Good, Stu thought. A man like The Snake would spot a fake easily, but maybe his men would not.

---

1   **bonnet** – *(AUS, BE) Motorhaube*
2   **to mess with sb.** – *versuchen, jdn. reinzulegen*
3   **to irritate sb.** – *jdn. verärgern*
4   **in fact** – *eigentlich*

After a minute the man nodded, and The Snake smiled.

Stu turned back to the sports car, the tension and the cocaine making his heart race.

He had almost reached the car when he heard The Snake speak again.

"Wait there a second, Stu," The Snake said, and Stu turned around, ready to dive to the floor. "Listen, I like a man who can keep cool under pressure. How about you give me a call in a few days, and we talk about doing some more business together?"

Stu felt a smile spread[1] across his face. "Sure, that would be fine."

The Snake grinned. "Good. Like I said, I've got a good feeling about you, Stu. I think you're gonna go far."

Stu nodded and watched as The Snake got back into the jeep and drove away towards the horizon.

Only then did the two criminals begin to laugh.

"Did you hear that, Duggie? He says I'm going to go far. The bloody idiot! Although, I guess he's right: I am gonna go far. Far away from him and this bloody desert! Let's get the hell out of here before they realise it's fake."

Duggie grinned. "Sounds good to me."

Stu was still laughing when he turned the key in the ignition of the car. Only when the engine failed to start did he stop.

"Bloody hell!" he heard Duggie say.

He tried it again, but there was only the dead, lifeless sound of a broken engine.

"What are we gonna do, Stu?" he heard Duggie say. "Stu? What are we gonna do?"

Stu tried the ignition one more time then sat back in the baking-hot heat of the car.

"Stu? There's no phone signal out here. What are we gonna do? Stu?"

---

1   **to spread –** *sich ausbreiten*

"Just let me bloody think!" Stu shouted.

And it was then, and only then, that he felt the first bead of sweat form on his usually bone-dry forehead. It rolled with an agonizing lack of speed down his shallow cheeks and fell from his chin to land on his shirt.

"Stu?" Duggie asked again.

But this time Stu had no answer.

Wolfe-Creek-Krater, Große Sandwüste, Australien

> Die Wüste **Great Sandy Desert** liegt im Nordwesten Australiens. In ihrem nordöstlichen Teil befindet sich der Wolfe Creek, ein 300.000 Jahre alter, von einem Meteoriten versursachter Krater. Wissenschaftler schätzen die Masse des Meteoriten auf etwa 50.000 Tonnen und seine Aufprallgeschwindigkeit auf ca. 54.000 km/h. Der Durchmesser des Kraters beträgt knapp 900 m.

In der Großen Sandwüste bewegen sich die Durchschnittswerte der sommerlichen Tagestemperaturen zwischen 38 und 42 Grad Celsius, im Winter zwischen 25 und 30 Grad.

Todesfälle sind auf abgelegenen Strecken durch die Wüste schon vorgekommen, wenn Reisende bei der Durchquerung wegen einer Autopanne zu einem unvorhergesehenen Halt gezwungen waren.

14. MURDER IN
THE DARKNESS

The darkness was cold, consuming and complete; however, the silence was not.

At first, when the lights had failed, there had been gasps[1] of panic and muttered reassurances that everything was okay.

As the seconds had become minutes, however, the darkness had filled not only the carriage[2] of the train but also the hearts and minds of the passengers, and the voices had faded to almost nothing.

Yet it was not just fear of the darkness that had silenced the voices, although this had undoubtedly contributed to the shared tension. No, it was the thought of where they were. The thought of why that darkness was so cold, consuming and complete.

The thought of the tunnel which surrounded them.

So in the darkness they sat and they waited, and there was still the occasional hushed[3] voice saying that the lights would return in just a moment. However, the thoughts of the people in the carriage were all of one thing.

They were thinking about the tunnel.

They were thinking about how deep and dark the tunnel was. They were thinking about the enormous weight of the sea above them.

For this was no ordinary tunnel. It was a thirty-one-mile-long tunnel buried two-hundred-and-fifty feet[4] beneath the sea.

It was the Channel Tunnel.

1   gasp – *Keuchen*
2   carriage – *Wagen*
3   hushed – *gedämpft*
4   foot – *Fuß (0,3048 Meter)*

And there was a quiet sense of dread[1] within the almost empty carriage of the passenger train.

Nick's mind rewound[2] an hour or so to the moment where he had boarded the train at St Pancras station. It was a cold February evening, and the air was decorated with a thin fog which had covered the glass ceiling of the terminal.

Taking his seat by the window, he stared at his reflection for a moment, noticing the dark rings under his eyes and running a hand through his chestnut hair to straighten it.

Idly[3], he turned to the few passengers sharing his carriage, inspecting their faces and guessing at their characters to pass the time.

In the far corner there was a thin and elderly woman, a book in her hand and a delicate lace hat[4] upon her head. A grandmother journeying to France to see her grandchildren, perhaps? Or a widow returning to the place where she had first met her late[5] husband?

On the table opposite the elderly lady, an American couple were talking about their trip to London, commenting on everything from the quaint[6] little houses to the high price of a ticket on the Underground.

Nick turned away from them to look at a younger couple on the next table. The man was flicking through[7] a newspaper, and the woman was reading a French phrase book. Occasionally, the woman would let her eyes move from the phrase book to the ring on her left hand. Then she would smile and look up at the man.

1	**dread –** *Grauen, Furcht*
2	**to rewind –** *zurückspulen*
3	**idly –** *träge*
4	**lace hat –** *Hut aus Spitze*
5	**late –** *verstorben*
6	**quaint –** *urig*
7	**to flick through sth. –** *etw. durchblättern*

Nick smiled too. It was easy enough to guess that they were going on their honeymoon.

Behind him he heard two men conversing in an eastern European language that he could not identify. Turning his head, he saw that they were both wearing dark suits and had serious expressions on their tanned faces. For a moment Nick watched them, trying to decide which country they were from. Then one of the men noticed him, and both stopped talking, their eyes focusing on him with an intensity that made him look away.

He was about to take a book from his bag when he noticed a woman in a black leather jacket boarding the train. She looked at her ticket and then spoke in French to the attendant[1] who directed her to a seat at the back of the carriage.

For a moment Nick watched her, but then, not wanting to annoy her too, he turned back to his coffee.

On the platform the conductor[2] looked at his watch, and then raised his whistle to his lips.

"Wait!" a voice shouted. A slightly overweight man in a white shirt and smart[3] black trousers was running to catch the train. His thin blond hair was a mess, and his round face was covered in sweat.

With an expression of annoyance the conductor signalled for him to be quick, and the man jumped onto the train with a small black briefcase in his right hand.

Curious, Nick watched as the man looked back at the platform as if he was expecting to see someone. Then, with a satisfied smile he hit the button on the door to the carriage and entered, breathing hard with sweat soaking[4] his white shirt.

As the man began to walk along the aisle[5], he turned his head quickly from side to side, noticing the faces of the other

---

1   **attendant –** *Zugbegleiter*
2   **conductor –** *Schaffner*
3   **smart –** *schick*
4   **to soak –** *durchnässen*
5   **aisle –** *Gang*

passengers. When he saw the two men in dark suits watching him, he stopped for a moment, an expression of fear moving across his face. Then the men turned away, and he continued to move along the aisle until he reached the table opposite Nick's.

"Just made it," Nick said as the man fell back into one of the seats.

The man turned to look at him, his hand moving to the black briefcase. "What?" he asked with a look of suspicion[1] in his eyes.

"The train. You only just[2] made it."

The man's expression softened, and he smiled. "Yeah, only just."

Then the conductor blew his whistle, and the train began to move, its slow rhythm gently encouraging Nick towards sleep.

As his eyes began to shut, he suddenly realised that he had seen the man at the next table somewhere before. Was he a writer? A musician? Nick was not sure.

But anyway, did it really matter? Because in less than two hours the man would be dead.

"Ladies and gentlemen…" The polite French accent of the attendant woke Nick from a light sleep.

At first he thought that they had already reached Paris, but then he noticed the nervous expressions on the faces of the other passengers.

"Why have we stopped?" asked the young man with the newspaper.

"It's nothing to worry about, I assure you. We have a small technical problem, and we have had to stop the train for just a few minutes."

"What kind of problem?" asked the American, a tall man with a bald head and pink cheeks.

MURDER IN THE DARKNESS

---

1   **suspicion –** *Misstrauen*
2   **only just –** *gerade noch*

"A minor problem with the electronics. Everything will be resolved in a moment."

"And where exactly are we? Under the bloody channel. Great place to break down," said the younger man again.

"Don't, James," said his wife.

"Sir, we have not broken down. The engine is fine; we just need to make a small repair," the attendant looked around at the nervous faces. "However, despite the fact that it is only a minor problem, we may lose the electricity in the carriages for a few minutes."

"Jesus Christ!" said the American. "You mean we're going to have to sit here in the dark?"

"For the briefest of moments, yes, but then the emergency lights will activate. And I can assure you it will take no more than a few minutes for the repairs to be completed."

There were no more questions, and the attendant took the opportunity to quickly retreat.

Leaning back in his seat Nick heard the man with the black briefcase at the next table swear. "Just when I thought I was out of the bloody country!"

"I'm sure it won't take long," said Nick.

"Yeah, well I know what will help with the wait," the man replied. Then, quickly turning the dials[1] on the lock of his briefcase, he opened it and removed a small silver hip flask[2]. "Best whisky money can buy," he grinned, and then he opened the flask and drank deeply. "Want some?"

Nick smiled. "I'm okay, thanks."

The man shook his head. "It won't kill you."

Then the lights flickered, and Nick looked around the carriage at the nervous faces.

"I think everything's okay," James said.

And that was when the darkness descended upon them.

1 **dial** - *Ziffer*
2 **hip flask** - *Flachmann*

Yes, the darkness was cold, consuming and complete, but the silence was not.

In fact, as Nick listened, he was sure that he could hear someone moving.

Someone creeping[1] along the carriage.

Someone breathing not far from him.

He turned his head to the left. Was that the shape of someone standing in the aisle by his table?

Someone waiting, watching?

Or was it just the dread of the tunnel, and the darkness playing tricks on his mind?

"Hello?" he asked. "Is someone there?"

And that was when the scream filled the silence.

It was a horrible sound: long, loud and barely human.

Panicked voices exploded from every part of the carriage, and Nick desperately pushed himself back against the window. "Lights!" he shouted. "Someone use a light. A phone, a torch, anything!"

"I've got my phone!" he heard James reply.

"Quickly!" Nick said, listening to the hurried movements in the darkness, sure that someone was moving towards him, trying to silence him.

But then the emergency lights activated, and the scene was drenched[2] in their strange glow.

Nick looked around.

There was no one in the aisle.

There was no one moving towards him.

"Who was that? Who screamed?" the American asked. "What the hell happened?"

Nick stood up. "I don't know. I think..." he began to say. But then he saw the body.

---

1   **to creep** – *kriechen*
2   **drenched** – *durchtränkt*

The eyes were open in a horrible expression of shock. Other than this, though, the man in the white shirt looked perfectly normal.

Apart from the small black knife protruding[1] from his chest.

"Jesus Christ!" said the American. Then his wife looked too, and another scream filled the carriage.

Nick watched as one by one the different passengers saw the body. The young couple were silent but horrified, both of them moving from their seats to stand in the aisle. The elderly lady looked at the knife then fell back into her seat, the Americans moving to help her as she fainted[2]. Behind him the two men in dark suits were talking, their expressions hard to read, and at the far end of the carriage the French woman was standing, her eyes moving across the faces of the other men and women.

"We've got to get out of here, Sian!" James said to the young woman, pulling her to the end of the carriage and hitting the button for the electric doors at the end of the aisle to open. "It's not working!" he shouted, hitting the button again.

"What do you mean?" asked the American.

"I mean it won't open! What else can that mean?"

"This one isn't working either," said the French lady from the other end of the carriage.

"What's... what's happening?" asked the elderly woman as her eyes flickered open.

"It's okay," Cherie, the American's wife, said, moving to her and holding her hand. "There's been... an accident."

"Accident?" said her husband. "The man's got a knife in his chest! Someone's murdered him!"

The words cut through the panic, and for a moment there was silence.

"Murdered?" repeated the elderly lady, but then her eyes rolled back into her head as she fainted again.

---

1   **to protrude from sth. –** *aus etw. hervorragen*
2   **to faint –** *ohnmächtig werden*

"Larry! Don't say that!" Cherie shouted at her husband.

"But he's right," said the French woman. "And there's something else which you should consider[1]."

Nick looked at her. "I know."

"What?" asked James. "What do you know?"

"Think about it. The lights went out because they cut the electricity to do the repairs."

"So?"

"So that's why the doors won't open either. They cut the power, the lights went out, the doors locked... and this man was murdered. Which means," continued the French woman, "that the murderer is still in this carriage." She looked around at the other passengers, watching their faces. "The murderer is one of you."

For a moment no one replied as each person searched the faces of the others.

"What the hell do you mean 'one of you'?" Larry shouted. "You're in here too! It could be you!"

The French woman shrugged. "Yes, but I know that it wasn't me."

"Look, we have to be calm about this," Nick said. "It won't be long until the electricity is turned on again. We just need to wait."

The French woman nodded. "I agree."

"Be calm? Wait?" asked James. "You just told us that someone in here is a murderer. Are we supposed to just wait until they kill someone else?"

Nick shook his head. "I don't think that's going to happen."
"Why not?" asked the French woman, taking a cigarette from her pocket and lighting it.

"Er, I don't think you can smoke in here," said Cherie.

"And I don't think you can kill people either, but look" she said and nodded at the body.

---

1   **to consider sth.** – *etw. in Betracht ziehen*

Behind him Nick could hear the two men in suits quietly talking, and he saw Larry look at them suspiciously. "What the hell are those two jabbering[1] about?"

The two men stopped talking, and one of them turned to Larry. "Excuse me?"

"Oh, so you do speak English. Maybe you could speak a bit more of it."

The man's expression turned cold. "I speak English, but my colleague does not. And tell me, why should I speak English? Why don't you try speaking my language?"

Larry wiped the sweat from his head and sat down.

"You said you didn't think anyone else would be killed," asked the French woman. "Why?"

Nick shook his head. "I don't know. There was something about this guy. When he got onto the train, I remember thinking that he looked nervous."

"What?" asked James. "Like he knew someone wanted to kill him?"

"Maybe not kill him, but something." Nick looked at the dead man's face again, and that feeling that he recognised him returned. "Does anyone know this man?"

Larry shrugged. "You were the one talking to him."

"No, I mean, his face. Is it familiar?"

Everyone turned to look at the body, but one by one they turned their eyes from him.

"Wait!" Sian said, standing up and staring. "I do! I recognise him. He was in James' newspaper!"

James moved back to their table and picked up the forgotten paper. "Jesus, you're right. He's here on the second bloody page.

"Who is he?"

---

1 **to jabber –** *quasseln*

"It says he's some ex-butler for some upper-class family. Jesus, yeah, it says this family is basically an extended part of the royal family. Some of the richest people in the country."

"Why ex-butler?" asked the French woman, extinguishing[1] her cigarette beneath her shoe.

"It says the family suspected him of stealing but could never prove it."

"So what does all this mean?" Larry asked. "It doesn't explain who killed him."

James shook his head. "It might, actually. The article says this guy claimed[2] to have some photos of the eldest son of the family. Apparently these pictures show him doing some pretty awful things, and they could ruin the family's reputation forever."

Nick looked at the dead man, and then let his eyes move to the black briefcase.

"The pictures must be in the case. If we can see them, maybe we will know who killed him," and he looked around at the others. "Does anyone disagree?"

There was a feeling of tension in the carriage again now, but no one spoke. He turned to the two men in dark suits and waited until the interpreter nodded his head in consent.

"I suppose waiting would have been boring," the French woman said. She moved down the aisle towards them. Larry and Cherie got up from their seats and stepped closer too.

"Who'll open it?" asked Sian.

Nick shrugged. "I'll do it, if I can get this lock open."

"Try this," James said, passing him a small penknife[3] that was attached to his keys.

Nick looked around once more, sure that whoever wanted the pictures to remain secret would say something.

MURDER IN THE DARKNESS

---

1   **to extinguish sth. –** *etw. auslöschen*
2   **to claim sth. –** *etw. behaupten*
3   **penknife –** *Taschenmesser*

Then, turning the case towards him he slid the small blunt[1] knife between the first lock and twisted it, the metal breaking easily.

"You know," said James. "Whatever is in there could make us rich."

Nick shook his head. "I just want to know who killed him."

He put the knife under the second lock and was about to turn when suddenly the emergency lights flickered.

"Jesus, if they turn off too..." James began.

Then the darkness swallowed them once more.

The first scream he heard was Sian's. Nick was sure of that, but he did not know if it was the loss of the lights or something much worse. The second scream, however, came from Larry.

And it was a scream of pain.

All around him voices filled the darkness with fear and panic; then something hard hit him around the head, and he fell back, dizzy and confused.

"The briefcase," a voice shouted. "Get the briefcase!"

Nick felt hands push him away, but he was angry now, the anger suffocating the fear. He swung his right arm, but there was nothing there. He swung the left, and his fist smashed against skin and bone.

"Bastard!" a voice shouted in the darkness.

"Lights! James, get the lights!"

For a moment there was nothing, but then bright white lights appeared from James' phone and then from Sian's and the interpreter's.

The scene was chaotic.

James had been pushed to the floor, and there was blood on his head where it had struck a table. Larry was lying on two seats and groaning, another small knife pushed into his shoulder.

---

1   **blunt –** *stumpf*

And in front of Nick, his nose pouring with blood, was the train attendant.

"You?" Nick shouted. "Why?"

The attendant shook his head. "She paid me! She said all I had to do was cut the lights and make it seem like the doors were locked. She said no one would know. That no one would suspect her, and she would escape and never tell anyone I helped. I needed the money you see."

"She?" Nick spun round, his eyes scanning the carriage.

Both sets of doors were now open.

And the French woman was gone.

"James, keep him here." Nick ran along the aisle and through the carriage doors. He then stopped and stared out of the open exterior door[1].

It was dark out there, the only illumination[2] provided by dim grey lights, and he had no idea if the French woman was waiting for him with another knife.

For a brief moment he hesitated. Then he jumped out of the door into the tunnel, turned to his left and ran into the darkness.

"Where are you going?" he heard the French woman say from behind him.

He turned to her slowly, raising his own hands and expecting to see a weapon in hers.

"Ha!" she laughed. "You thought it was me? How gullible[3] you are. I felt her push past me. I didn't know who it was until I caught her out here. I suppose my face probably looked as shocked as yours."

Nick lowered his hands and shook his head. "I don't believe it. Why?"

---

1   **exterior door** – *Außentür*
2   **illumination** – *Beleuchtung*
3   **gullible** – *naiv*

The elderly woman was silent for a moment, her arms held firmly behind her back by the French woman. Her lace hat was gone, and her thin dark hair was a mess. By her feet was another knife which Nick guessed the French woman had taken from her.

When she spoke, her voice was cold and bitter. "Why? You ask me that?" she shrieked[1], her tone hinting at some type of mania. "That man deserved to die. He was a thief and a liar. More than that, though, he betrayed one of the oldest and noblest families in the country. I would do it again in an instant."

"Who are you?" asked Nick. "You can't be part of the family or he would have recognised you."

The woman shook her head, her old eyes half-crazed[2]. "Oh, but I am part of the family. One of the most important parts. I looked after the boy like a mother. I protected him from scum[3] like that dead man all his young life. And yes, they took my job from me when they said I was too old, but that doesn't mean I just give in[4]. It doesn't mean I just stop loving him. I had enough money saved up to pay that idiot attendant to stop the train. I would have paid every penny I had. Because I knew the family would thank me. I knew my little lord would thank me. Because I could kill that thief and go to prison, and the family could keep its reputation."
Nick shook his head again.

"Englishman, it's not hard to see, is it?" the French woman said with a raised eyebrow. "Our sweet little old lady is our rich lord's nanny."

1   **to shriek** – *kreischen*
2   **crazed** – *wirr*
3   **scum** – *Abschaum*
4   **to give in** – *aufgeben*

Calais, Frankreich

Für den Channel Tunnel (Deutsch: Eurotunnel) gab es bereits im
18. Jahrhundert erste Ideen, wobei diese damals noch die Fortbewegung
mittels Pferdekutschen vorsahen mit einer Insel in der Mitte des durch
Öllampen erleuchteten Tunnels, die dem Tausch der Pferde dienen
sollte.

1987 begannen die Arbeiten am Tunnel, an denen insgesamt
13.000 Arbeiter, Techniker und Ingenieure beteiligt waren. Nach der
Fertigstellung 1994 war es zum ersten Mal seit dem Ende der letzten
Eiszeit vor über 13.000 Jahren möglich, trockenen Fußes vom
europäischen Festland nach Großbritannien zu gelangen.

Der Eurotunnel ist im Laufe der Jahre immer wieder Ausgangspunkt für
zahlreiche Flüchtlinge, die durch den Tunnel ins Vereinigte Königreich
gelangen wollen, indem sie versuchen, auf LKWs und Güterzüge zu
klettern. Dabei kommt es immer wieder zu Todesfällen.

WORTLISTE

	a handful	eine Handvoll
	a horrific scene	ein Bild des Grauens
	a trail ends cold	sich als kalte Spur erweisen
to	abuse sb.	jdn. misshandeln
	abused	Missbrauchsopfer
	ad	Anzeige
	addict	Süchtige(r)
	aimed at sb.	auf jdn. gerichtet
	aisle	Gang
	ambassador	Botschafter
	amount	Menge
	and that was that	und das war's
	angle	Erklärung
	annoyance	Ärger
	anticipation	Vorfreude
	antidote	Gegengift
	anxiety	Unbehagen
to	approach sth.	sich etw. nähern
	armed	bewaffnet
	arson	Brandstiftung
	as though	als ob
to	assess sb.	jdn. mustern
to	atone for sth.	für etw. büßen
	attempted murder	versuchter Mord
	attendant	Zugbegleiter
	auburn	rostrot
	audition	Vorsprechen
	authority	Behörde
to	awake	aufwachen
to	bang against sth.	gegen etw. stoßen
not to	be allowed to do sth.	etw. nicht machen dürfen
to	be convicted of a crime	eines Verbrechens überführt werden
to	be devoid of sth.	an etw. mangeln
to	be in no rush	es nicht eilig haben
to	be in one's prime	im besten Alter sein
to	be mistaken	sich irren
to	be the one	der/die richtige sein
	beacon	Leuchtfeuer
	bead	Schweißtropfen
	bead of sweat	Schweißperle
to	beat	schlagen
to	bet	wetten
	binoculars (pl.)	Fernglas
to	blame sb. for sth.	jdm. etw. verübeln
to	blaze	funkeln
	blind drunk	stockbetrunken
	blinding	blendend grell
	blistering	glühend
	bloodshot	blutunterlaufen
	blunt	stumpf
	body	Leiche
	bone dry	knochentrocken
	boot	(BE, AUS) Kofferraum
to	bounce back	zurückspringen
	bound	Sprung
	box	Loge
to	bring sb. to justice	jdn. vor Gericht bringen
	bruise	Bluterguss
	bullet-proof vest	schusssichere Weste
	burn	Brandwunde
to	call for sb. to do sth.	jdn. auffordern, etw. zu tun
	capacity	Potential
	carriage	Wagen
to	catch sth.	etw. erblicken
	chained	angekettet
to	claim sth.	etw. behaupten
	closet	(AE) Kleiderschrank
	coffin	Sarg
to	come to do sth.	dazu kommen, etw. zu tun
	competitor	Konkurrent

to	compose oneself	sich zusammen-nehmen	
	condo(minium)	(AE) Eigentums-wohnung	
	conductor	Schaffner	
to	confess	ein Geständnis ablegen	
to	consider sth.	etw. in Betracht ziehen	
	constable	Polizist	
	convict	Verbrecher	
	cop	(AE, ugs.) Bulle	
	copycat killer	Nachahmungs-täter	
	corner shop	Tante-Emma-Laden	
	counterfeit money	Falschgeld	
	crack	Spalt	
to	crack a case	einen Fall lösen	
	crackle	Knistern	
	crazed	wirr	
to	creak	knarren	
to	creep	kriechen	
	crime syndicate	Verbrecherbande	
to	crouch	kauern	
	crown court	Strafgerichtshof	
	dashboard	Armaturenbrett	
	deafening	ohrenbetäubend	
	death anniver-sary	Todestag	
	deed	Tat	
	defiant	unnachgiebig	
	demeanour	Auftreten	
	derelict	verlassen	
	devout	fromm	
	dial	Ziffer	
	dialled number	gewählte Nummer	
	Did he hell!	Nie im Leben!	
to	disappear into thin air	sich in Luft auflösen	
	disgraced	blamiert	
	disgust	Ekel	
to	dismiss sth./sb. from one's thoughts	etw./jdn. ausblenden	
	disquieting	beunruhigend	
	distaste	Abneigung	
	domed	gewölbt	
	domestic abuse	häusliche Gewalt	
	Don't be silly!	Red keinen Unsinn!	
	Don't you dare!	Wage es nicht!	

	double-crossing	hintergehend
	doubtless	sicherlich
to	down a drink	ein Getränk aus-trinken
to	downsize	schrumpfen
	dread	Grauen, Furcht
	drenched	durchtränkt
	driveway	Einfahrt
to	drop off sth.	abliefern
to	drop sth.	etw. fallen lassen
	dull	stumpfsinnig
	edge	Kante
	effort	Bemühung
	encounter	Begegnung
to	encourage sb. to do sth.	jdn. zu etw. ermutigen
	expat	im Ausland leben-der Mensch
	exterior door	Außentür
to	extinguish sth.	etw. auslöschen
to	fail to do sth.	etw. nicht machen können
to	faint	ohnmächtig werden
	faith	Glaube
to	fall for sb.	jdm. verfallen
to	familiarise oneself with sth.	sich mit etw. ver-traut machen
to	feel a stab of jealousy	einen Anflug von Eifersucht verspüren
	fella	Kerl
	female lead	weibliche Haupt-rolle
	filing cabinet	Aktenschrank
	filthy	dreckig
	flammable	leichtentzündlich
to	flash sth.	etw. aufblitzen lassen
to	flick through sth.	etw. durchblättern
	flock	Gemeinde
	foot	Fuß (0,3048 Meter)
	fortified wine	Dessertwein
	foster family	Pflegefamilie
to	frame sb. for sth.	jdm. etw. an-hängen
	furious	zornig
	gambling addiction	Spielsucht

	gasp	Keuchen	
to	get all the way	durchkommen	
to	get sth. wrapped up	etw. eingetütet bekommen	
	ghastliness	Grässlichkeit	
to	give in	aufgeben	
	glad	froh	
to	go	sterben	
	goddamn	verdammt	
	gorgeous	umwerfend	
	grill (of a car)	Kühlergrill	
	grim	düster	
	grin	Grinsen	
	groin	Leiste	
to	growl	knurren	
	guilt	Schuldgefühl	
	gullible	naiv	
	guts	Bauch	
	hammer of the pistol	Hahn	
to	handcuff sb. to sth.	jdn. mit Handschellen an etw. fesseln	
	handkerchief	Stofftaschentuch	
not to have a clue	keine Ahnung haben	
	haze	Dunst	
to	head towards sth.	sich auf etw. zubewegen	
to	heave	würgen	
	Here's to you.	Auf dein Wohl.	
	hip flask	Flachmann	
to	hit the bar	(ugs.) zur Bar gehen	
	homicide	Tötung	
	horrendous	entsetzlich	
	housemate	Mitbewohner	
to	hover	schweben	
	How dare you?	Wie können Sie es wagen?	
	hunting lodge	Jagdhütte	
	hushed	gedämpft	
	I might as well...	Ich könnte ebenso gut...	
	I would hear...	Ich hörte immer ...	
	I would rather...	Ich würde lieber...	
	idly	träge	
to	ignite	anzünden	
	illumination	Beleuchtung	
	impatience	Ungeduld	
	impenetrable	undurchdringlich	
	in distress	in der Not	

	in fact	eigentlich	
	in spite of	trotz	
	incendiary	Brandmittel	
	indeed	durchaus	
	infamous	berüchtigt	
	infamously	berüchtigt	
	influence	Einfluss	
to	inherit sth.	etw. erben	
	injury	Verletzung	
	ink cartridge	Tintenpatrone	
	inquest	Untersuchungsausschuss	
	insane	verrückt	
	insistent	eindringlich	
to	irritate sb.	jdn. verärgern	
	item	Gegenstand	
to	jabber	quasseln	
	jet-black	samtschwarz	
	junk	Ramsch	
to	keep one's temper	Ruhe bewahren	
to	key sth. in	etw. eingeben	
to	kneel down	sich hinknien	
	lace hat	Hut aus Spitze	
to	lament over sth.	über etw. klagen	
	late	verstorben	
	lead	Hinweis	
to	lean down	sich beugen	
to	leave sb. alone	jdn. in Ruhe lassen	
not to leave a spot	sich nicht vom Fleck rühren	
	length	Länge	
	lenient	nachsichtig	
	lid	Deckel	
	Like father like son.	Wie der Vater, so der Sohn.	
	loan request	Darlehensantrag	
	lobby	Eingangshalle	
	lock-up	(ugs.) Gefängnis	
	lodge	Hütte	
to	look forward to sth.	sich auf etw. freuen	
	lumberjack shirt	Holzfällerhemd	
	luminous hands	Leuchtzeiger	
	madman	Verrückter	
	magnifying glass	Lupe	
	malicious	bösartig	
	malignant	bösartig	
to	matter	von Bedeutung sein	

	mercy	Gnade	to	purchase	erwerben, kaufen
to	mess with sb.	versuchen, jdn. reinzulegen	to	put a fire out	ein Feuer löschen
	messed up	versaut		quaint	urig
	metal spring	Metallfeder		questioningly	fragend
	mirage	Fata Morgana	to	race	pochen
	misery	Elend		real player	führende Figur
	mistrust	Misstrauen		reed	Schilf
	moan	Stöhnen		regret	Reue
	mob	Mafia		reinforced glass	drahtverstärktes Glas
	mobster	Gangster		reputation	Ruf
to	mock sth.	etw. verspotten	to	resist	Widerstand leisten
	moron	Depp	to	retch	würgen
	moth	Nachtfalter	to	rewind	zurückspulen
	muffled	gedämpft	to	rip into sth.	etw. zerreißen
to	mute	dämpfen		ripped	zerrissen
	neat	ordentlich		rock	(ugs.) Edelstein
	nerves (pl.)	Nervosität		ruined flesh	zerfetztes Fleisch
	next of kin	nächster Angehöriger		ruling	Richterspruch
				sacrifice	Opfergabe
	nope	nö		saviour	Heiland
	oak	Eiche	to	scramble	hasten
	odd	seltsam	to	scribble	kritzeln
	oncoming	entgegen- kommend		script	Drehbuch
				scum	Abschaum
	one's true self	jds. wahres Ich		sense of impending doom	Vernichtungs- gefühl
	only just	gerade noch			
	opposite	gegenüber		Shame.	Wie schade.
	outskirts	Stadtrand		shotgun	Flinte
	pamphlet	Broschüre	to	shriek	kreischen
	pants	(AE) Hose	to	slur sb.'s voice	jds. Stimme undeutlich machen
	peat bog	Torfmoor			
	penknife	Taschenmesser			
	perimeter	Stadtrand		small-time	mickerig
	perpetrator	Täter		smart	schick
	petty criminal	Kleinkrimineller	to	soak	durchnässen
to	picture sth.	sich etw. ausmalen		soaked	pitschnass
	pile	Stapel		soil	Erde
	pill	Tablette		soundproof	schalldicht
to	plunge sth. into sth.	etw. in etw. hinein- stecken		Speak of the devil!	Wenn man vom Teufel spricht!
	poison	Gift			
	porch	(AE) Veranda		speaking of which...	da wir gerade da- von reden, ...
to	praise sb.	jdn. loben			
to	prescribe	verschreiben	to	spike a drink	etw. in einen Drink tun
to	protrude from sth.	aus etw. hervor- ragen			
				spontaneous combus- tion	spontane Ver- brennung
to	pull an insur- ance job	einen Versiche- rungsbetrug begehen			
			to	spread	sich ausbreiten
to	pull oneself together	sich zusammen- reißen		stack	Stapel

to	stagger	schwanken	to	tie sb. up	jdn. fesseln
	starved	ausgehungert		to-die-for	unwiderstehlich
	steering wheel	Lenkrad		toast	Trinksrpuch
	stew	Eintopf		troubling	beunruhigend
	stock	Aktie	to	twist	sich drehen
	straight away	sofort		tyre	Reifen
	strap	Riemen		unbelieving	ungläubig
	streak	Strähne		unconscious	unbewusst
to	strike	schlagen		untouchable	unantastbar
to	strike sth.	gegen etw. schlagen	to	upset sb.	jdn. durcheinander bringen
	striking	auffallend		upstanding	aufrecht
	striking similarity	verblüffende Ähnlichkeit		vacant	ausdruckslos (Blick)
	struggle	Kampf		vaguely	annähernd
	studiously	sorgsam		vault	Tresorraum
	stunned	verblüfft		vengeance	Rache
	subtle	dezent		virtually	praktisch
to	suffocate	ersticken		warden	Gefängnisdirektor
to	suit sb.	jdm. gut stehen (Kleidung)	to	wash over sb.	jdn. überschwemmen
	suspicion	Verdacht, Misstrauen		whereas	während
				white lie	Notlüge
	swamp	Sumpf		width	Breite
to	sway	schwanken		will	Testament
to	swear	fluchen	to	wipe one's hands on sth.	sich die Hände an etw. abwischen
to	swerve	ausscheren			
to	take over	die Führung übernehmen		wire	Wanze (Abhörgerät)
to	take revenge upon sb.	sich an jdm. rächen		with disdain	verachtungsvoll
	talkative	gesprächig	to	wonder	sich fragen
	tapped in the head	verrückt		wounded	verletzt
				wrist	Handgelenk
to	tear into sth.	sich über etw. hermachen		yard	Yard (0,914 Meter)
	thud	dumpfer Schlag		You take care.	Pass auf dich auf.

Mörderische Kurzkrimis zum Englischlernen

BILDQUELLEN

Umschlag:
Aktentasche: /Thinkstock/RTimages; Auge: shutterstock/dean bertoncelj

S. 3 (Dominic Butler): Dominic Butler; **S. 6-7, Weltkarte:** shutterstock/Tetiana Yurchenko; **S. 14, The Angel of the North:** shutterstock/Alastair Wallace; **S. 22, Grand Canyon:** shutterstock/RRuntsch; **S. 29, Folsom Prison:** shutterstock/Keith McIntyre; **S. 36, Hollywood:** shutterstock/Atomazul; **S. 43, Oil platforms, Cromarty, UK:** shutterstock/ZRyzner; **S. 51, Fairbanks, Alaska:** shutterstock/Gary Whitton; **S. 59, King John Castle, Limerick:** shutterstock/Patryk Kosmider; **S. 67, Ottawa, Canada:** shutterstock/Click Images; **S. 74, Royal Albert Hall:** shutterstock/Neil Mitchell; **S. 81, New Zealand, North Island:** shutterstock/Tupungato; **S. 88, Statue of Liberty:** shutterstock/T photography; **S. 96, Sun City, South Africa:** shutterstock/Athol Lewis; **S. 103, Wolf Creek, Great Sandy Desert:** shutterstock/David PETIT; **S. 117, Calais:** shutterstock/David Hughes.

TEXTQUELLEN

S. 88, „The New Colossus": Emma Lazarus.